Coffee Shop Conversations

*Making the Most
of Spiritual Small Talk*

Dale Fincher
Jonalyn Fincher

This is helpful, thoughtful, culturally savvy guidance for spiritual conversations. Read it and learn.

John Ortberg, author and pastor,
Menlo Park Presbyterian Church

Coffee Shop Conversations is refreshing, bold, and engaging. Dale and Jonalyn have done a wonderful job of highlighting the importance of genuinely engaging people in meaningful spiritual conversations in the manner and spirit of Jesus.

Sean McDowell, speaker, educator, and author of
Apologetics for a New Generation

Coffee Shop Conversations is really not a book about talking. It's a compilation of personal stories that demonstrates how to listen to non-Christians with empathy. It's a timely book for evangelicals, one that shows us how to love without compromising truth and holiness.

Sarah Sumner, PhD, dean,
A. W. Tozer Theological Seminary

Read *Coffee Shop Conversations* if you want to engage in interesting, provocative dialogue about your faith and journey. The Finchers are bright, thoughtful, and great conversationalists. The evidence is in story after story of fascinating encounters with all kinds of people, and they handle them with grace and truth.

Dick Staub, host of *The Kindlings Muse* and
author of *The Culturally Savvy Christian*

No message is more important than this: the God of the universe knows all about you, and he loves you and forgives you. Every person touched by that good news should want to share it with others. Why don't they? Sometimes, it's simply this: nobody has coached them how to do it in a natural and unpretentious way. *Coffee Shop Conversations* provides a way for all Christians to make the gospel clear and accessible to everyone. The Finchers' style of evangelism is both self-aware and empathetic. I highly recommend this book for all who take Jesus' command to make disciples seriously. I will be using this book in my evangelism courses.

Jerry Root, PhD, associate professor of Evangelism and Leadership at Wheaton College

My roommate is quite openly gay and quite openly confused about religion in general. We've had many great discussions, but some of the points from chapter 3 — the conversation stoppers — spoke so well to what we talk about. The combination of personal experience and theological background is so helpful for me for our future conversations! This book is applicable to such a wide spectrum of people because, despite the fact that religion is one of those "no-go" conversation topics, it is very much talked about. This [book] offers people the skills to make a spiritual conversation a little easier, and hopefully less offensive, harsh, and heated, but more informational and caring.

Ally Packer, Peace Corps worker

Coffee Shop Conversations completely changed my viewpoint and helped so much with discussions about God. I have a friend who is having challenges with her abusive ex-husband and doubting her beliefs. We have had some beautiful and open discussions thanks to knowledge gained from reading this new book!

Laura Brock, homeschooler, Steamboat Springs, Colorado

Coffee Shop Conversations helps us talk about the REAL Jesus.

Jon Hale, nurse, Seattle, Washington

Coffee Shop Conversations has given me courage and confidence that I have something really worth sharing. It's spoken to me on my present personal journey to love people in my life that I have been pushing away.

Ellyn Myller, administrative assistant, Steamboat Springs, Colorado

Coffee Shop Conversations

Coffee Shop Conversations

*Making the Most
of Spiritual Small Talk*

Dale Fincher
Jonalyn Fincher

ZONDERVAN®

ZONDERVAN.com/
AUTHORTRACKER
follow your favorite authors

ZONDERVAN

Coffee Shop Conversations
Copyright © 2010 by Charles Dale Fincher and Jonalyn Grace Fincher

This title is also available as a Zondervan ebook. Visit www.zondervan.com/ebooks.

This title is also available in a Zondervan audio edition. Visit www.zondervan.fm.

Requests for information should be addressed to:
Zondervan, *Grand Rapids, Michigan* 49530

Library of Congress Cataloging-in-Publication Data

Fincher, Dale.
    Coffee shop conversations : making the most of spiritual small talk / Dale
Fincher and Jonalyn Fincher.
        p.   cm.
    Includes bibliographical references.
    ISBN 978-0-310-31887-3 (softcover)
    1. Evangelistic work. 2. Conversation — Religious aspects — Christianity.
I. Fincher, Jonalyn Grace, 1979 - II. Title.
    BV3793.F475   2010
    269'.2 — dc22   2010001880

All Scripture quotations, unless otherwise indicated, are taken from the Holy Bible, *Today's New International Version*™. *TNIV*®. Copyright © 2001, 2005 by Biblica, Inc.™ Used by permission of Zondervan. All rights reserved worldwide.

Scripture quotations marked NASB are taken from the *New American Standard Bible*. Copyright © 1960, 1962, 1963, 1968, 1971, 1972, 1973, 1975, 1977, 1995 by The Lockman Foundation. Used by permission.

Scripture quotations marked MSG are taken from *The Message*. Copyright © 1993, 1994, 1995, 1996, 2000, 2001, 2002. Used by permission of NavPress Publishing Group.

Any Internet addresses (websites, blogs, etc.) and telephone numbers printed in this book are offered as a resource. They are not intended in any way to be or imply an endorsement by Zondervan, nor does Zondervan vouch for the content of these sites and numbers for the life of this book.

Published in association with the literary agency of Alive Communications, Inc., 7680 Goddard Street, Suite 200, Colorado Springs, CO 80920. www.alivecommunications.com

Cover design: Jeff Miller, Faceout Studio
Interior design: Sherri L. Hoffman

Printed in the United States of America

10 11 12 13 14 15 /DCI/ 22 21 20 19 18 17 16 15 14 13 12 11 10 9 8 7 6 5 4 3 2 1

To our grandparents

D. D. & Velma Davis
Mary Taylor
George & Grace Latapie

Whose ordinary lives with Jesus
Look extraordinary in the world.

———————

Contents

Preface: *A Coffee Shop Conversation*   11
Introduction: *Humble Confidence*   13

Part I: Making Spiritual Small Talk

1. What Is My Neighbor?   19
2. Loving Discourse   34
3. Conversation Stoppers   52
4. Jesus: The Way, the Truth, and the Good Life   63

Part II: Restocking Your Tools

5. How to Read the Bible   73
6. Lost Words   100
7. Misquoting Jesus   118
8. One True Religion   128
9. The Hope for Human Healing   148

Part III: Helping Friends Home

10. Mountains That Are Molehills   161
11. Molehills That Are Mountains   173
12. God Talk ,   196
13. Talking about the Resurrection   207
14. Happy to Be Human   216

Notes   223

"Be wise in the way you act toward outsiders; make the most of every opportunity. Let your conversation be always full of grace, seasoned with salt, so that you may know how to answer anyone."

Paul to the church in Colossae

Preface

A Coffee Shop Conversation

Traveling in Tennessee, we stop for drinks at a coffee shop. Standing in line, a tall, lovely woman with short curly hair smiles at me (Jonalyn)[a] and says, "Great haircut."

"Thanks, I love your curls!" I tell her.

"Yeah, thanks. I was thinking of a new way to get mine cut ..." She fingered the curls at the nape of her neck.

"You could *totally* do this," I say.

"I used to have long hair, but I had to cut it really short because of this illness." Her voice trails off, then she brightens. "But I like yours. I've seen that style in magazines, but now I see what it looks like on someone's head."

"Yeah, like 3-D." We smile.

After a quick glance at the overhead menu she asks, "Do you live here?"

"No, we're from Colorado, in town for business."

"What do you do?"

"My husband and I run a nonprofit."

"What kind of nonprofit?"

"It's called Soulation. We help people have healthy souls."

"Awww, wow! That's neat."

"Yes, very rewarding. I'm speaking at a church tomorrow." I tell her the name. "Heard of it?"

---

[a] To keep the book easy to read and conversational, we've written each line together. If we personally tell a story, the narrator "I" will be identified in parentheses (Dale or Jonalyn).

She shakes her head, "I don't know where that is. I'm still kind of new to this area." She pauses, lowers her voice, and says, "It's so different here than from where I'm from—the Northeast."

"Yep, it *is* very ... um, *Christian* here," I add.

"Exactly. I'm not used to this at all."

"Sometimes Christian culture can be almost ... repressive."

"Yeah." She looks grateful.

"You said you had an illness ...?"

"Oh, it was so involved, encephalitis. I mean, I recovered and was recuperating so well. Then, they said I'd have to cut off all my hair because of an infection."

"How frustrating!"

"It really was! I felt so vain for caring about it so much, but ..."

"I think hair is really important to women."

"I wish people realized that!" she chimes.

"You know, there's this wonderful Jewish proverb that says, 'Hair is a woman's glory.'"

"That's interesting. I've never heard that."

"It's one of my favorites from the Bible," I add."[b]

The cashier asks for my order. I step forward and order, then glance to my left and say, "Have fun growing your hair out!"

She smiles as we head for our table. "Thanks!"

---

[b] 1 Cor. 11:15.

Introduction

Humble Confidence

You know what's really unattractive about Christians?" our artist friend Jeff once said to us. "They're always on a mission. Too many Christians think they have nothing to gain from others except to get them saved. I don't like it when *anyone* has an agenda and is not visiting with me straight up. Why can't they stop, pay attention, and listen?"

We've asked ourselves the same thing. Author Anne Lamott writes in her spiritual memoir, *Traveling Mercies*, "Most Christians seem almost hostile in their belief that they are saved and you aren't."[1]

In his letter to the church in Colossae, Paul taught to be wise in the way we act toward those who believe differently from us, to make the most of every opportunity by conversing in ways full of grace.[a] When we moved to a small house in the woods, we noticed how the chipmunks scurried out on a mission, only to hurry back to their hole. Chipmunks remind us of the way we used to approach evangelism, treating people as mission projects, scurrying out to them only to

Chipmunks remind us of the way we used to approach evangelism, treating people as mission projects, scurrying out to them only to hurry back to the safety of our den.

---

[a] Colossians 4:5–6.

hurry back to the safety of our den. This is *not* making the most of every opportunity.

For several years, we've been growing into a new way of conversing that is helping us listen without scurrying away. Every person, we believe, has something to teach us about life. While we believe Jesus distinguishes himself as the Savior and King of us all, while we obey his teachings because we believe they give us the best road map for life, we also believe the biblical idea that all humans—be they Christians, Buddhists, Mormons, atheists—are made in God's image.[b] All humans reflect God in varying degrees of clarity. Therefore we approach every conversation as fellow learners rather than posturing as experts. We can gather data and truth even from those who do not follow Jesus, growing in wisdom and love, and giving others dignity by assuming they are doing the same. If we want our conversations to always be full of grace, then humility, not deft arguments or clever words, must become our first concern.

Many biblical men and women listened and loved others without compromising their friendship with the God of Israel.

Jesus struck up conversations with humility. When he spoke with a pagan outcast—the Syro-Phoenician woman—he was open to her interruption and even let her challenge his theology.[c] Paul did too. He mingled in the marketplace, which informed his speech on Mars Hill. He talked about the Creator and Judge and listened for hours to pagan responses.[d] Abraham's servant shared in such a respectful way that he won his pagan listeners over without ever insulting their religion.[e] Esther saved the Jewish nation by submitting to the cultural rules even as she questioned the law of the pagan king.[f] Many biblical men and women listened and loved others without compromising their friendship with the God of Israel. They humbly listened to those who crossed their path

---

[b] Gen. 1:27. [c] Mark 7:24–30 MSG. [d] Acts 17:16–22. [e] Genesis 24:12–51. [f] Esther 7:4; see also Esther 4:12–5:8; 7:1–4; and 8:16.

because they knew that even a capricious prophet riding a talking donkey might have something to teach them about their God.[g]

We realize it is risky to allow others to influence us, especially if they do not recognize the Scripture as God's truth or follow his laws. But God promises that if we anchor ourselves to the truth and love of God, we remain free to listen and love without danger of walking astray. The Lord is our shepherd who protects us. In 2 Timothy, Paul wants the young leader to understand, "The Spirit God gave us does not make us timid, but gives us power, love and self-discipline." In the same passage Paul writes, "I know whom I have believed, and am convinced that he is able to guard what I have entrusted to him until that day."[b] He will guard our souls as we lovingly listen and navigate different views of spirituality today, from yoga to goddess worship.

A healthy spirituality always draws us to the person of God, but this doesn't mean we close our ears to learning. As we develop a view of the universe and our human place in it, we remain grounded by putting Jesus at the center. After challenging conversations we regularly revisit Jesus' way of seeing things. Why did Jesus want people to know the Father? What is Jesus' view of creation-care? Does Jesus care about emotional health? How would he respond to evangelists knocking at our door? Who would he have time for? Who would elicit his judgment? His mercy? How would he act in marriage? How would Jesus raise children or love his in-laws?

A truly spiritual person cultivates a life of love. A Christian spiritual person will know the love of Jesus and his point of view.

As we converse with those who claim other forms of spirituality, we must be grounded enough in our own to show them a shining alternative. Spirituality is not merely about meditation, morning Bible reading, or church attendance. A truly spiritual person

---

[g] Numbers 22.   [b] 2 Timothy 1:7 and 11.

cultivates a life of love. A Christian spiritual person will know the love of Jesus and his point of view.

With the aid of Jesus, we want to season our conversations with open-hearted grace. The goal of this book is to help us make friends for the journey and to talk with humble confidence about God without sounding pushy or feeling befuddled, infusing even the briefest interaction with meaning.

Small talk might seem straightforward, but not every topic will be easy—either to discuss in these pages or to practice in daily conversation. We want to help you understand why certain topics distract our friends from ever discovering why we love Jesus—topics like evolution, hypocrisy, hell, and homosexuality. We'll get a clearer view of the mountains we see as molehills and vice versa. Feel free to jump to chapters that catch your interest, but keep in mind that every chapter is loaded with perspectives and tools that have dramatically helped us make the most of our spiritual small talk.

We hope our experiences of conversation with friends inspire you to try out a more refreshing way to talk about spirituality. Our prayer is for you to grow wiser and more humble, to give good news, and to spread the friendship of Jesus and the love of God.

Part I

---

*Making Spiritual
Small Talk*

Chapter 1

What Is My Neighbor?

We both grew up in a tradition keen on evangelizing. Following a grandparent's example, I (Jonalyn) applied a litmus test question for all my new friends. "If you were to die tonight, do you know where you'd go?" I read soul-winning guidelines and tracts that promised to get people saved without them suspecting a thing. I proselytized out of fear for my friends' eternal destiny. On the surface I was successful: many of my friends converted.

I (Dale) also used similar tactics explained by my Christian school teachers. Layered on top of my concern that my friends were headed to hell, I was motivated by guilt. If I didn't share immediately and directly, I would disappoint God and miss my sole purpose as a young Christian. I spent most of my formative years in Christian culture riddled by a feeling of failure.

We've come to wonder how many of our friends, when "conversions" did happen, prayed the sinner's prayer to soothe our evangelical fervor. Rarely did we witness a truly changed person. For most, even after the appropriate prayer and the congratulations of an elated youth group, Jesus was no more alive in our friends' daily lives, romantic hopes, college plans, or friendships than he was before. In fact, once a friend "converted," Jesus barely ever re-entered our conversation. We'd done our job, they'd done theirs, and the memory was slightly embarrassing to revisit.

Winning a fast-track conversion by simply telling someone that "Jesus saves" is less honest and even easier than sharing what Jesus really means in our lives. If we admit that Christianity is no picnic, and that Jesus often leaves us walking in mysteries, two surprises await us. First, we'll ask ourselves many of the same questions that only "nonbelievers" are supposed to ask. Second, we'll discover that our friends listen longer and with genuine interest. An open, personal dialogue with our friends is most likely when we open a window into our own souls, confessing doubts and disappointments with God. Honesty makes spiritual conversations work.

Winning a fast-track conversion by simply telling someone that "Jesus saves" is less honest and even easier than sharing what Jesus really means in our lives.

Non-Christians

Most of us are scarcely willing to imagine the help and comfort non-Christians' current beliefs give them. We don't realize why a Wiccan finds hope in the Goddess, because we never asked or listened to her story of how she felt when she learned God was exclusively male. We don't realize that the Buddhist monk treasures Buddha's instruction to avoid touching women because he's personally witnessed sexual perversion in the church he used to attend. We remain ignorant about the spiritual hunger of those we meet because we fail to get to know them.

In the past, I (Jonalyn) have often struck up conversations on plane trips and noticed my internal stress as I find out my neighbor's religion. If my neighbor mentions church or God I relax, feeling like I'm with someone I don't have to convert. But if my neighbor lets on that she's spiritual but not religious, or angry at God, or any other non-Christian flavoring, I feel a tangible tightening in my stomach.

I have believed that next to me sits an "unbeliever" who needs to be saved, and until she accepts Jesus, she is a danger both to me and others. My Pavlovian reaction makes conversation awkward and agenda-driven from the start. In some cases I find myself believing that non-Christians are actually societal threats capable of shredding family values, corrupting morality, voting liberal, and mocking everything for which I stand. If I befriend them without saving them first, I might be corrupted by them! So I gear up to share the salvation message.

Most of us are scarcely willing to imagine the help and comfort non-Christians' current beliefs give them.

Perhaps you can relate to the fevered feeling to share Christ and discharge your duty. Perhaps you've ended up saying things that prove you don't really care to listen, like, "Jesus hung on Calvary for your sins" — as if the listener knows what Calvary means or who Jesus is or what sin is.

On one popular radio show we heard recently, professional apologists tried to bully college students into conversion by berating them with the Ten Commandments and the question, "How have you broken these?" The apologists followed up by pushing into the young people's lives with questions like, "Have you ever lusted after a woman? Jesus says that's the same as committing adultery with her in your heart." At this point most of the students excused themselves. Some explained they were Buddhists or atheists; some confessed their disbelief in the Bible.

Regardless, the apologists dismissed the students' point of view, ending any hope for mutual respect in the conversation. We heard the apologists announce the universal need for a savior and smoothly introduce Jesus and the "plan" of salvation. Few, if any students, accepted Jesus. It didn't matter; the radio host praised this apologist for his boldness and the method as a great way to witness and stand up for your faith. We groaned because we used to do the same thing.

One honest friend admits that talking about his faith is like intellectual arm wrestling. "If I don't crush them, I've lost. If I budge toward them, they've won." Evangelism is not arm wrestling, where we have to clench our teeth and monologue our point of view because we're afraid of losing, afraid this unbeliever might win the argument. Talking about Jesus isn't a contest.

For years we thought sharing our faith meant saying the right things to get people saved. But whenever we treat our friends as problems to solve or objects to fix, we are not relating to them as people. As one wise man said, "You can't have a relationship with someone if you're objectifying them." Women don't want men objectifying them as trophies; neither do our friends want us objectifying them as potential converts.

For years we thought sharing our faith meant saying the right things to get people saved.

Perhaps we never risk sharing Jesus, because we know from experience that Christians already have a bad reputation for being pushy about their faith. We grow understandably nervous around non-Christians so we never utter a word about our faith, trying to be a good example, hoping they'll ask us a question one day. If our friend is hostile to religion, we carefully avoid any talk about God for fear of giving offense. Sometimes we simply have no idea what to say to someone so different from us.

Categorization and Calcification

We all once lived in a world without hard categories defining others and their beliefs. In *An American Childhood*, Annie Dillard reminds us of the ways we saw the world as children. Dillard is five when she realizes a world outside her window connects with her own. "Men with jackhammers broke up Edgerton Avenue. When I lay to nap, I listened. One restless afternoon I connected the new noise in my bedroom with the jackhammer men I had been seeing outside. I understood abruptly that these worlds met, the outside and the inside."[1]

I (Dale) remember my own days connecting those dots, smiling when I discovered that the same mall we arrived at by car could be reached through back alleys on my bike. Or when I saw Mrs.

Carver, my fourth-grade teacher, eating at a restaurant and dressed in street clothes. I discovered, to my surprise, that my teacher could appear in public, that she could live beyond the decorated walls of her classroom.

As children, when surprises jolt us, we simply adjust to the reality. When we're young, we bend ourselves to the changing shape of our world. But somewhere around junior high, the world's fluid categories begin to solidify. We begin to place people into boxes: jock, popular, nerd, pretty, gay, straight, the sick kid, the rich kid, the troublemaker.

As children, we were quick to reassign categories based on the steady inflow of new information. We had no choice; we had to assimilate. As adults, however, we resist modifying our categories. We surround ourselves with friends who affirm our calcified opinions. Our views of science, politics, money, class, and religion—of how things *ought* to be—are reinforced by the denomination or church small group we join. We justify our hard-line stances with our education and even our own interpretation of Scriptures. When our categories become more important than the people *in* the categories, we have become thoroughly modern adults who know how to justify our distance from our neighbor.

When my (Dale's) mom fought cancer, she remarked, "I'm not a cancer patient—I'm a person who has cancer!" By this point my mom had lost all her hair. She wore a wig, not for her own vanity, but to help people uncomfortable with her baldness. When her wig irritated her head, she'd whip it off without warning. She was right: people categorized her as a bald lady, as a cancer patient, as a dying person. But she was a *person* first, eager to keep living life.

> *Our views of science, politics, money, class, and religion—of how things ought to be—are reinforced by the denomination or church small group we join.*

The reason we need to hold our categories loosely is not that categories are inherently bad, but that often our categories are incorrect. We file people in the wrong places and leave them there. Yet a child's humility teaches us to willingly bend to fit the world. Walling people into categories prevents us from loving them.

Social psychologists tell us we make up our mind about someone in minutes — all the more reason to consciously hold our categories loosely over the course of a life. If we label a teen as a misfit, we may be unable to learn from his insights about teen culture, and we may be cursing him with a label he feels unable to change. If we avoid a cancer patient because we find her depressing, we cannot learn her road of suffering. If we think of an elderly man as obsolete as he slowly writes a check in the grocery line, we cannot allow his slow pace to question our frenzied overachieving. If we think of a Sikh as someone who needs converting, we cannot learn what she believes about God. Unless we get to know our neighbors beyond their labels, we cannot make the most of our spiritual conversations with them.

In grammar school, I (Jonalyn) met Sakina, a girl from a Sikh family. Though I knew nothing about Sikhs, I knew they were not Christians, which meant their religion was wrong. I realized I might be her only chance to get to heaven.

My friends and I soon learned from Sakina that Sikhs should never cut their hair. That set Sakina apart from us, and we revered her unsheared baby ringlets hanging way down on her back. I admired her willpower and envied the length, a living Rapunzel. But mixed with my admiration was scorn. How silly to think that long hair could make you holy!

During craft time, I worked with a pair of scissors. Sakina was engrossed in her project directly in front of me, her black curls brushing my desk. I nudged my friend Heather and play-motioned snipping off one of those ringlets. Heather pulled my brandished arm away. "You can't do that," she whispered fiercely in my ear. "You'd get her in so much trouble. Don't you know about her religion?"

"I know," I replied flippantly. "I was just joking."

I had put Sakina in my non-Christian box. That stunt was my little way of proving that her religion was a load of hooey and that long hair didn't matter to *my* God. I imagined myself producing the cut curl and sermonizing to her that Jesus didn't care about long hair, but that he *had* died for her. And with snipped tresses, she'd have to leave Sikhism anyway, right? A foolproof witnessing plan!

A Label-Defying Jesus

Jesus didn't act like many modern evangelicals. When Jesus met people, he dignified their search for the good life, giving them parables to mull over and offering winsome, playful banter when they could handle his verbal sparring.[a] Adults shunned children, but Jesus scooped them into his lap.[b] When his culture considered women irrational and the private property of men, Jesus educated women and counted them among his closest friends.[c] When the religious laws abused people, Jesus looked behind the law at God's intention to give life and health.[d] When people had a faulty theology, he gently offered his living water.[e]

In Jesus' world, everyone distinguished between two groups, male Jews who God loved and everyone else—Gentiles, Samaritans, tax collectors, women, and children. Today we still make distinctions of who is closer and further from the love of God, like moral Christians living in suburbs and morally questionable types like drug-addicts, homosexuals, Unitarians, politicians, or the sexually promiscuous. But Jesus overlooked his culture's hard-and-fast categories to love morally questionable types. He was dangerously attractive to the outcasts in his society. Both Jewish and non-Jewish masses followed Jesus—divorcees, adulterers, prostitutes, IRS guys, the weak, the demon oppressed, and the diseased. He loved them beyond their labels, seeing them as people, bearing the image of God.

Those outside the church often understand this category-bending humility better than those who claim to follow Jesus.

---

[a] Matthew 13 and Mark 7:24–30. [b] Matthew 19:13–14. [c] Luke 10:39. [d] Mark 12:38–44. [e] John 4:11–15.

Recently, secular feminists pushed many in the church to fully consider women as valuable as men in every walk of life—causing the church to remember Jesus' view of women. Politically correct cries for tolerance can seem closer to the heart of Jesus' love than Christians who joke about "gays" or "retards." The secular concern with diversity may be more effective in inviting crowds awaiting fish and loaves than our derisive glances at those who don't fit our categories of social, sexual, ethnic, and religious acceptability.

We can change the messages we send in our spiritual small talk— words that are empathetic, openly thoughtful, and culturally savvy.

The recent book *unChristian* by David Kinnaman and Gabe Lyons paints a clear picture of Christians' reputation today: homophobic, intolerant, overly political, sheltered, hypocritical, and judgmental. This message humbles us, to be sure, but we can change the messages *we* send in our spiritual small talk—words that are empathetic, openly thoughtful, and culturally savvy. We then can begin to scrape the canvas clean and create a truly inviting picture.

Changing the way we do spiritual small talk begins with relearning our audience. Since church authority and traditional church attendance no longer claim people's loyalty, Americans are turning to their own forms of spirituality. How do we talk with someone who has created a one-of-a-kind religion?

The Birth of Spiritual Designers

The Pew Forum on Religion and Public Life reported in June 2008 that the number of people creating their own interpretations of faith and culture is growing. While 92 percent of Americans believe in God, less than half are confident in what God is like. These statistics validate what we see on high school and college campuses, at the mall, in coffee shops, and even among churchgoers all over the country.

Spirituality is on the rise; religion is declining. Krista Tippett, radio host of National Public Radio's *Speaking of Faith*, explains that today's religions are "the containers of faith—malleable and corruptible in the hands of people who fashion and control them." Today people see spirituality as "faith's original impulse and essence," a way to relate to God without human ideas or corrupted texts getting in the way.[2] Many relate to God in spiritual, but not religious, ways, customizing their spirituality. As author Anne Lamott puts it in her memoir of finding Jesus, "Mine was a patchwork God, sewn together from bits of rag and ribbon, Eastern and Western, pagan and Hebrew, everything but the kitchen sink and Jesus."[3] We call this "spiritual designing." Spiritual designers find the spiritual traditions, practices, and creeds that best fit their needs, and many hold to their newly minted spirituality with the same fervor for exclusivity and persuasion as any committed Christian or Muslim.

How can we tell if a person designs their own spirituality?

Spiritual designers are more concerned with relating to God than following doctrine. Suspicious of organized religion, they invest their time hunting for experiences of God rather than accepting theology from a religious authority. Often they will choose the type of spiritual beliefs and practices that feel most comfortable to them, borrowing from mutually exclusive religions. They find connection with God or their higher power through a cornucopia of channels. Some feel more spiritual when they chant or beat drums, others when they eat organic or vegan, others when they wear semiprecious gems, others when flying colorful prayer flags. Some tune into the frequency of the divine by visiting exotic places to sit under a yogi, others by uncovering secret meanings and decoding messages in nature or other holy books. Other spiritual designers cling to God through symbolic images, like dangling a cross from their rearview mirror. We've met many spiritual designers who call themselves "Christians" too.

Often spiritual designers are peace-keeping people reaching for a quieter, natural life, more concerned with balancing with

Spiritual designers are more concerned with relating to God than following doctrine. nature than pursuing technology. Spiritual designers, however, like all religious people, assume the world would be a better place if others discovered the same spiritual point of view. They search, like we all do, for love strong enough and truth compelling enough to embrace for life. A good conversation begins when we see them as fellow humans hungering for love as much as we are.

A Human Who Needed Love

One afternoon before we were married, I sat in a grocery store parking lot arguing with Dale. We had compressed all our wedding planning into three months, so every day included specific, time-sensitive deadlines. Dale's to-do list that day included making key calls and adding names to the guest list—but he had dropped the ball. In my mind, this was unacceptable.

I attacked him with my words, cutting him down, blaming him for incompetence and for ruining not just my afternoon, but *my* wedding. Did he even *want* this to work out? Now *I* would have to pick up after him.

After my verbal assault, Dale sat quietly. I could see pain in his eyes. I expected he would scold me or tell me I couldn't talk to him like that, but he didn't. After a long pause, he asked softly, "Jonalyn, is that how you talk to yourself?"

His question stunned me. I could scarcely manage to nod as tears spilled down my cheeks. Sitting in the car in that parking lot, I wept long and hard. For the first time I realized how my unkindness grew from the root of fear that I was not good enough. I was so accustomed to living with self-imposed pressure to be a model Christian woman that I couldn't love or enjoy the love of those around me.

My behavior toward Dale sprung from my fears about God, whom I had designed to be exacting and ungracious. I was demanding because I had designed a God who was demanding. I berated myself because it was the only way I knew how to motivate myself.

Dale saw the wounded person behind my judgmental words and showed me something about following Jesus that I had never experienced: I could fail and still be accepted. Only in receiving love without conditions could I know how to give unconditional love. Even though I had claimed Jesus for twenty years as my "personal Lord and Savior," I finally began to taste Jesus' love like this.

In Jesus' eyes I wasn't merely a flustered fiancée, a blamer, or a fearful, controlling person. Jesus and Dale looked beyond that and saw me as a human who needed love.[4] This is the way Jesus would have us share love with others, especially spiritual designers. We get to look beyond their different beliefs and into their human souls to see our shared struggles.

We get to look beyond their different beliefs and into their human soul to see our shared struggles.

In America, many of our friends already have inklings about Jesus, but they haven't tasted his love. As we talk with our friends, whoever they are and wherever they come from, we want to move them to experience God's love. "No one has ever seen God; but if we love one another, God lives in us and his love is made complete in us."[f] We are an arm of God's love. "In this world we are like Jesus."[g] We cannot underestimate the way our stories of God's love to us allow our friends to entertain the hope that God loves them too.

People Packages

All people are like packages. God invites us to look beyond the outside labels and give people our attention. Jesus shows us how to open the envelopes of people's lives and know our neighbors beyond the roles they play. Like the wrapping, our bodies conceal

---

[f] 1 John 4:12.   [g] 1 John 4:17.

our souls within. Each person holds unknown surprises, unique concerns, interests, and motivations. What's inside the packages we call people?

Often we mistakenly assume we know a human package because of a label like *mom, president, teacher, prayer warrior.* A person is more than the car they drive, the job they serve, the family they come from, the religion they follow. Too often we think we know a person because we know a few of their roles. But a person is more than what they do.

> *A person is more than the car they drive, the job they serve, the family they come from, the religion they follow.*

People are like money; they exist beyond the roles they play. Notice those green bills you carry around as currency. When you hand over a few dollars to pay for groceries, you have not handed over money; you've handed over pieces of paper with green ink. That's all a dollar bill literally is, though we've agreed as a society to use these greened papers to exchange goods. That's why they all say, "Federal Reserve Note"; they're worth something as long as our federal system holds. We could cut a bill into strips to use as bookmarks and it would still remain paper with green ink, but it would no longer be currency. Notice the difference between what a dollar bill *is* and what a dollar bill *does*.

In the same way, observe the difference between what people *are* (a human made to reflect God) and what they *do* (their job or label). For instance, the kind nurse, Cynthia, we met at the hospital is more than a nurse. She could quit practicing medicine, but she would still be Cynthia, body and soul. As we talked with her, we glimpsed what was inside, her natural, human concerns. She fears God's anger toward her for living with a man she never married. That lawn man we talked with last week isn't only a lawn guy. He is Pedro, who works three jobs and wishes his oldest son was not running with a rough crowd. Pedro just happens to be pushing a rotor over manicured grass. Our neighbor Elisa, who drapes Buddhist prayer flags from tree to tree, is not merely a Buddhist; she could convert to another religion and still be Elisa. At core, she is a human who happens to believe that her karmic debt is heavy from poor decisions in her twenties.

We would love people better if we looked beyond their labels and opened the package of their souls. Though our conclusions differ, we can learn from British secular writer Karen Armstrong, who recommends that when we study any new religious idea, we ought to "keep on asking, 'But why? But why?' ... until you come to the point where you can imagine yourself feeling the same."[5]

> *Will we label the couple next door based on their Hanukkah display, or will we get to know them and discover their daily fear for their son's safety in Iraq?*

Why does our neighbor flirt and smirk and scowl? What makes her eyes gleam with anticipation? Who makes her feel safe? What comforts, fears, or questions does her religion bring to her? Will we label the couple next door based on their Hanukkah display, or will we get to know them and discover their daily fear for their son's safety in Iraq? Do we know the reason our friend strings prayer flags from her balcony? Beneath and inside their spirituality, *who are they?*

Who are *we?*

What Is Our Neighbor?

Today we ask the same question that the law student asked Jesus, "Who is our neighbor?"[b] In today's American conversations, this question often assumes we identify our neighbor by the role they play. In other words, when we answer "Who is my neighbor?" we might say, "Oh, she's a Buddhist," or "He's a gun fanatic," or "She's a business owner." "Who are they?" often means, "What do they do?" and "Where are they from?" We know we're supposed to love

---

[b] Luke 10:29.

those different from us, but we continue to think about them primarily through the label, which dims our vision of them and who they can become. How often we have found ourselves labeling our neighbors, "That's our street's busybody!" or "Lucy's always a ditz," or "Those Mormons," or "Crazy David." We must change our private language to clean the lens through we which we see them by asking first, "*What* is our neighbor?"

We know we're supposed to love those different from us, but we continue to think about them primarily through the label, which dims our vision of them and who they can become.

Jesus answers the law student's question about neighbors with the story of the Good Samaritan, a man whose humility springs from recognizing a beaten body as a human. The priest and Levite passed by an unclean, Jewish victim, but the Samaritan stopped for a fellow human.[i] As Christian essayist and author Madeleine L'Engle writes, "The root word of *humility* is *humus*, earth; to be *human*, too, comes from the same word."[6] Instead of asking *who* our neighbor is and slapping on a label, we must ask the deeper, less obvious question first, "*What* is my neighbor?" Our neighbors are human and, like us, made of earth. We are all "but dust," as the Psalmist says, but we all live because of God's breath.[j] We share the same dependence on our frail bodies, the same concerns and hopes for this life, and the same wondering hope for life beyond the grave.

An Invitation to Be More Human

When we make a habit of seeing others not by their labels, but by their humanity, we give them a taste of God wooing them. They learn they are valuable for what they *are*, not for what they can *do*, nor what they believe; they understand the first premise of the

---

[i] Matthew 19:19.   [j] Psalm 103:14; Psalm 104:29; Genesis 2:7.

gospel, "For God so loved the world," this world teeming with frail and glorious humans.[k] We're inviting them to notice their humanity as we have noticed ours.

We will introduce them to a God who wants to reclaim the original plan for humans. We are more than mere dust, more than wormy, sin-infested creatures. The incarnation of Jesus means that our humanity hasn't sunk so low as to be worthless to God.

Our humanity is a lost thing that has to be found. Jesus shows us what humans can be. He proves we need not always say, "I can't help messing up. I'm only human." Jesus pulled our humanity up from the depths, teaching us that our flaws arise from our fallenness, not our humanness.

Most people think Christianity focuses merely on good behavior, church membership, or going to heaven when they die, not on redeeming humanity. But God's essential reason for making humans was to create beings that reflected him, bright mirrors without spot or blemish.[l] He reaffirmed his plan when "the Word became flesh and made his dwelling among us." Madeleine L'Engle again explains, "As Christians we are meant to be not less human than other people but more human, just as Jesus of Nazareth was more human."[7]

Jesus showed us what humans are meant to look like; he incarnates God's original blueprint. We point our neighbors to Jesus, a model of what we all, with God's help, can become. Jesus invites us into a journey that ends with making us fully human.[m]

That's his plan, one that we constantly try to communicate. How do we have the kind of loving discourse that rolls out a red carpet to welcome our neighbors in?

---

[k] John 3:16. [l] Genesis 1:27. [m] Matthew 16:25.

Chapter 2

Loving Discourse

Our friend Natalie attended a silent retreat at a monastery where a woman named Anna confessed her growing faith in Wicca. Anna repeatedly interrupted Natalie's solitude to preach how the Catholic Church had corrupted all the true teachings of Jesus. Anna proselytized fervently, even insulting the Christian attendees for thinking the Scriptures could be trusted.

Natalie was suffering from a tight neck, so the first evening she silently prayed that one of the attendees would offer her a short massage. In the morning, Anna offered to work on Natalie's neck. Describing her gratitude, Natalie wrote:

> Who am I to turn away an answered prayer because the other person has a different set of beliefs? God provided for me and I told her so when she offered … She wanted to chatter, but most of it was about her life and feelings and exploring her nervous beliefs. I complimented her throughout the weekend, although she drove me nuts. We talked a lot. I think it was supposed to happen.

Natalie looks back on the retreat as a success. "I tried hard to be a light, loving and accepting. She hugged me because she said I was the first Christian who let her know that I was okay with her right to be a Wiccan. She said she didn't feel judged. I felt judged, but she didn't."

Natalie refused to label Anna as "that annoying Wiccan" to avoid. She treated Anna as a human. Natalie broke through Anna's condescension by following the manners of loving discourse.

Manners of Loving Discourse

We believe that timeless manners—respect, empathy, honesty, fair-mindedness, flexibility, vulnerability, and patience—preserve friendships and allow them to grow, even amid significant disagreement. Manners work best when they're two-way, but we are called to practice them with love and grace even if we do so alone. They should never be used to manipulate others.

> *Manners are ways to honor human dignity, foster smart dialogue, and protect each other's freedom of conscience.*

Manners are ways to honor human dignity, foster smart dialogue, and protect each other's freedom of conscience. Below we give you seven manners, in no particular order, needful for any spiritual conversations.

Manner 1: Respect One Another

Regardless of another's beliefs, and no matter how ludicrous their spirituality sounds to us, we have the duty and privilege to demonstrate respect. Because every human is uniquely made in the image of God, Jesus commands all his followers to equally value each Wiccan, Taoist, Buddhist, Muslim, and spiritual designer.

> *Differences in belief cannot make a human unworthy of our respect.*

Differences in belief cannot make a human unworthy of our respect. Even if a person despises Christians, treat them with the highest value that Jesus offers, for every person bears the image of God.[a]

---

[a] Genesis 1:27; Mark 6:34; Luke 6:29; Romans 12:18.

We can test our level of respect for others by noticing how we talk about non-Christians when we are with other Christians. Do we mock them? Do we ascribe unverified motives to them because of their beliefs? For instance, do we find ourselves suspicious that a neighbor is godless or deceitful because she had an abortion? Do we snicker at a co-worker who wears amulets and prays to the Goddess? Do we stereotype and denigrate gays with our lunchtime buddies?

If we are eager to talk about Jesus' sacrifice, we need to show them our own willingness to love them with sacrifice. We may find ourselves welcomed into someone else's life when we lay down our sword of ridicule. Mocking others, even behind their backs, destroys our capacity to respect them when we speak face to face.

The good news ends up looking more like a weapon from an enemy forcing others into a narrow religion, rather than an open-hearted offer of a road map to a fellow traveler.

As C. S. Lewis points out, real merriment can only exist between friends who take each other seriously—no flippancy, no superiority, no presumption.[1]

Respect entails godly tolerance, which allows us to say, "I'll be open with my journey; will you be open with yours? Maybe we can help each other find our way through this world." Tolerance of this kind offers to others what we've found to be good, true, and beautiful. It listens to what others have found. If we don't listen out of respect, we can talk about Jesus all day long and make no more sense than a clanging cymbal.[b] The good news ends up looking more like a weapon from an enemy forcing others into a narrow religion, rather than an open-hearted offer of a road map to a fellow traveler.

Paul modeled godly tolerance when he shared his faith, knowing that true persuasion stemmed from Jesus' love more than clever words.[c] In his letter to the Thessalonians he writes, "With the help

---

[b] 1 Corinthians 13:1–3.   [c] 2 Corinthians 5:14–15.

of God we dared to tell you his gospel in the face of strong opposition. The appeal we make does not spring from error or impure motives, nor are we trying to trick you … we never used flattery nor did we put on a mask to cover up greed."[d]

Paul saw the non-Christian Thessalonians as people who deserved the respect of honest dialogue — and as potential partners on the journey to know God. He stripped off any masks covering himself or his message.

We know godly tolerance means the Spirit of God is working in us, because godly tolerance means we love even when we feel offended. I (Jonalyn) speak and write regularly about women's value beyond the roles they're permitted to play. I believe deeply in women's partnership with men in home and church. So when a famous megachurch pastor met us in his green room shaking my hand, but commenting to Dale, "Nice looking wife," I felt intolerance bubbling up in me. I'd like to ask him to greet me personally, not just Dale. I'd rather not smile.

Because I care about women and justice, it's even harder to see things from his point of view, to remember his sexist comment was intended to compliment both of us. Tolerance means I interact with him, even though his words hurt. He may not see women as I do (as I believe Jesus does), but he is still human. Instead of parking on a strong confrontation that might destroy any fruitful interaction that may later persuade him with love, we both steered the conversation to find common ground. We engaged him with questions about his marriage, ministry, and goals.

Godly tolerance means we respect other's decisions. We refuse to withhold love from them because we dislike their views. We still try to persuade others, but caring more for our friend's conscience than converting them to our point of view. Paul writes, "Rather, we have renounced secret and shameful ways; we do not use deception, nor do we distort the word of God. On the contrary, by setting

---

[d] 1 Thessalonians 2:2–3, 5.

forth the truth plainly we commend ourselves to everyone's conscience in the sight of God."[e]

There is no biblical precedent for forced conversion, whether by the sword or peer pressure or manipulation (e.g., scaring teens with rapture movies as their sole basis to follow Jesus). Jesus gave people space to consider and follow him of their own free choice. He knew he was asking for their entire lives, and he didn't want hasty, fairweather disciples. Even when people chose another path, Jesus let them go and grieved.[f] Paul invokes the differences in our consciences when he recommends to the believers in Rome to let each fellow believer consult their own conscience about eating meat sacrificed to idols.[g] Even when Paul stands on trial before the Empire, his life or death dependent on his ability to convince the governing authorities of the power and person of Jesus, Paul refuses to use trickery, coercion, or manipulation. He simply tells his story.[h]

> *Jesus gave people space to consider and follow him of their own free choice.*

Whether people follow Jesus or not, we can trust that Jesus is working. The Hound of Heaven[2] pursues each of us, as evident in Jesus' words that he came to "seek and save what was lost."[i] Lost things are wanted things. Though many resist being friends of God, we still love them, scorning the very idea that they must convert to earn our continued interest. This is how Jesus treated his friends — even the one he knew would betray him.

Manner 2: Step into Their Shoes

When I (Jonalyn) reconnected on Facebook with a friend from junior high, I quickly discovered that she was "out" as a lesbian. In her email revealing her lifestyle, I knew I had a clear choice: end the dialogue out of my own discomfort or inquire into her life. She listed her cell number and invited me to call, so I picked up the phone and dialed.

---

[e] 2 Corinthians 4:2.   [f] Mark 10:17–23.   [g] Romans 14:22.   [h] Acts 26:1–31.   [i] Luke 19:10.

After an hour of catching up, I decided to ask her what I would have wanted to be asked if I lived her life. "What was it like sharing your sexuality with others? Was it hard for you to come out?"

She graciously shared, opening to me the contradictions and frustrations she lives with daily. At the end of our conversation my friend identified herself as a lesbian to me. I admit I was shocked when she said, "I'm just a big old dyke who loves others, but who is still afraid to tell people at times." She regularly challenges me to try to see the world from her perspective. She's given me much to wrestle with, since she loves Jesus too.

On her recommendation we rented *The Bible Tells Me So*, a film that explores the lives of gay people who also want to love Jesus. I now understand more about what she fears, what she needs, and what God's love has done for her. Because I value her as an image bearer of God, and since I could tell she was very nervous about sharing, I listened to her without revealing my own views about homosexuality. I could tell she wasn't ready to hear them. A few conversations later she affirmed my suspicion by telling me, "I can't ask your perspective yet. It would be too hard for me to hear." Currently, I have the joy of getting to know her without her fearing I will reject or fear her. She values my honest inquiry and has offered her friendship to me—a friendship that would be impossible if I was unwilling to step into her shoes.

We try to approach friends with the attitude of a learner. A friend might say, "I feel so much better when I'm done meditating, like my body is cleansed, like my mind is lighter." Here is a chance to step into their world. What specifically about meditation feels cleansing, for example? *Without needing to agree with their beliefs or practices, we are putting ourselves into another life in the same way Jesus put himself into ours.* Without needing to agree with their beliefs or practices, we are putting ourselves into another life in the same way Jesus put himself into ours. We are free to continue asking questions and learning: What experiences in your life (past or present) have made you realize you needed meditation? What makes meditation the place you find peace?

Listen without correcting or stockpiling rejoinders. Enjoy discovering the deep, personal needs of another. Love requires true listening, which as psychologist Scott Peck explains,

> Involves bracketing, a setting aside of the self, it also *temporarily* involves a total acceptance of the other. Sensing this acceptance, the speaker will feel less and less vulnerable and more and more inclined to open up the inner recesses of his or her mind.[3]

They may be saying something we need to consider for ourselves. They may not be. But we won't know until we try. Try to imaginatively put on their shoes, practicing the virtue of empathy, just as Daniel stepped into the shoes of his captors, the pagan Babylonians, learning their culture and language without neglecting his devotion to God in prayer.[j]

Walking in another's shoes means refusing to immediately pounce on any suspicious-sounding ideas. Digest their answers. Learn about their life and what they love about their spirituality. If this makes you uncomfortable or sounds dangerous, keep in mind that listening does not mean you also agree; it merely means you are willing to hear them fully. This is how we want people to listen to us.[k]

Even more, in our culture where spiritual designers create their own religion, we have to learn to listen; otherwise, we will never know what they believe. I (Jonalyn) shared Jesus with my agnostic friend during my first year at college. I would often jump up in the middle of a discussion to find her a book that better explained a point I was trying to make. During a foray into my library to find a perfect rebuttal, she interrupted me, "That's the

In our day, the individuals we befriend must educate us about what they believe.

---

[j] Daniel 1:3–4, 6:10.   [k] Luke 6:31.

difference between us. I can't show you a book of what I believe; there isn't any textbook that explains what I believe. I just create it as I go along."

In our day, the individuals we befriend must educate us about what they believe. We must step into *their* unique shoes and view *their* spiritual world from *their* perspective. We have found this worth our time, because such patient friendship is the only appropriate way to love each other.

Manner 3: Wrestle on Your Own

After I (Dale) gave a speech at a university, a student approached me. He felt like he needed evidence for God's existence or his love.

"Let's start with something simple," I said. "Do you trust your eyes and what you see?"

"Sometimes. But my eyes can be deceived too. I feel like we can't have any certainty in the world."

"Certainty is a tall order," I added. "But we can go with what makes sense, what is more reasonable to believe. Like, I have more evidence that you exist than that you're just a hologram. Following the bits of evidence seems more human than throwing out all evidence in a demand for certainty."

The student admitted he wanted what was reasonable. We hashed and rehashed ideas about truth that evening, and he and I continued our discussion online for many months.

I spent time thinking about his struggle, wondering about his real barrier to belief and asking myself the same questions he had. I felt his intellectual struggle, but in thinking as he did, I also saw a bulging door of pain waiting to be opened. He wasn't looking for more information, but to find something—anything—he could *trust*.

In my next email, instead of giving him more reasons, I asked him *why* he distrusted his own abilities, like sight, reason, intuition. A flood of hurts from parents, friends, and church came back to my inbox. He couldn't trust himself because he couldn't trust anyone, let alone God. Wrestling with his questions on my own helped me know how to engage him as the hurt person behind the intellectual query.

On our own time we ask ourselves, Do his ideas make sense? Does her religion help her get what she longs for, lasting relationships? Is he using religion to hide? Does his spirituality help him use his gifts? Wrestling with our friends' questions on our own for the sake of helping them provides good material to share when the conversation comes up again.

When we wrestle on our own and then present a question for everyone to work through, we can shift our position from the expert into the fellow learner. For example, my (Jonalyn's) book club recommended *The Four Agreements*, which taught a version of the Law of Attraction (the idea that a person's thoughts literally reshape the universe, for good or ill). Rather than state my opinion that the book abused Scripture and was not in keeping with Jesus' teaching, I asked a question about the Law of Attraction. "If this is true," I said, "then would I be responsible for causing my recent miscarriage?" That gave us lots to talk about, opening up an honest dialogue in which all of us were free to consider problems with the Law of Attraction.

Wrestling with ideas on our own gives our friends a chance to know we care about truth and love. Even if their view of life remains unchanged, in some quiet future moment they may remember that you loved them.

Wrestling with ideas on our own gives our friends a chance to know we care about truth and love.

Our call is to love people with God's love, even when they don't know it, by thinking about and working for their spiritual health on our own time. Jesus prayed for Peter to stand firm in his faith, even when Peter wasn't around.[l] On his own time Jesus loved us too, even thousands of years before we were born.[m]

---

[l] Luke 22:31–32.   [m] John 17:16–25.

Manner 4: Never Judge a Thing by Its Abuse

I (Dale) reclined at a pool on a lazy afternoon, surrounded by tourists with the same idea. The gentleman next to me asked where I was from and what I did. I had recently begun my masters in philosophy, so we started talking about philosophy and suffering, which led to how his mother had Alzheimer's disease and how much it bothered him. I offered some consolation that my grandmother suffered in the same way. I had recently read that perhaps Alzheimer's slowly separates the soul from a person's body, so I shared how, perhaps, his mother remained fully herself, but without a clear connection to communicate to him.

The idea of the soul provoked personal questions from which he learned I was a Christian. Fairly quickly he said, "The problem with Christianity is all those crusades, inquisitions, child-molesting priests. How can you believe in a religion that has hurt so many people in the name of God?"

His response distressed me. I've heard this argument against Christianity often. It's tempting to use the checkered history of any movement as a reason to dismiss it. However, as a friend once told me, we can't measure a thing by its abuses. Every philosophical idea, every religion, must be taken on its own merit, how the founder lived it, not based on how people have abused it or taken advantage of it. For us, we look to the life of Jesus. Did he promote reckless crusades or sexual abuse? Since he didn't, such objections don't stick to Jesus.

Every philosophical idea, every religion, must be taken on its own merit, how the founder lived it, not based on how people have abused it or taken advantage of it.

When people say they can't follow Jesus because of abuses by Christians, we sit with them and try to empathize with their list of offenses. When the appropriate time comes, we even share how bothered we are by some who call themselves Christians. We always end by sharing how we cannot measure Jesus by those who abuse him. We know this principle is true in other areas of our lives; for instance we still elect presidents even after Nixon, and we still use money despite Wall Street's abuses.

Of course, Christians need to heed the same wisdom. We cannot reject Buddhism as violent because some Tibetan monks went to war. Buddha taught nonviolence. We cannot reject Islam because our Muslim boss is having an affair. Muhammad taught faithfulness to your wife or wives. We cannot judge Mormonism as abusive because some Mormon men abandon teenage boys. Joseph Smith never advocated child abuse. We cannot reject atheism because Stalin killed millions. Atheism doesn't mandate mass murder. Choosing or rejecting a religion or belief system must hinge on the religious founder and his or her teachings, not subsequent abuse.

Choosing or rejecting a religion or belief system must hinge on the religious founder and his or her teachings, not subsequent abuse.

If we've considered Buddhists to be thieves because a Buddhist man was reported for embezzlement, we'd do well to ask another Buddhist if that is what Buddhism teaches. A conversation with a Buddhist will help us all consider a religion based on its real teaching.

A fair-minded person wants to get at the authentic religion before sharpening knives of criticism. When we know little about another religion, or when we think we know much from apologetic seminars or books, we are always glad to meet a devout follower to pepper with questions. We will ask them, "Why did you convert?" or "Why do you follow your God?" A conversation with committed followers of other religions often helps us properly analyze their religion for its own merit, and not by someone's abuses of it. Often without having to crack open a book.

Manner 5: Update Your Opinions of Others

We've all enjoyed the relief when a childhood friend takes time to realize we've changed for the better. In our family, we call this willingness to change our minds *updating*. Just like the programs in our computers, we need to update our opinions of others as we get to know them, as they change their minds and reveal more of themselves to us.

I (Jonalyn) have a longtime friend from college, Annie, whom I met my sophomore year studying abroad. When we met, Annie distinguished herself as a Marxist, feminist, Jewish agnostic. She and her boyfriend often joined me sightseeing in London. We all got along, though we filled most of our conversations with debating things like whether humans were basically good or evil. While we walked to shows, while we rode the Tube, I tried repeatedly to show her how deeply evil lived in us. Neither of us budged.

A decade later we remain friends, connecting when we happen to be in the same town. I've changed quite a bit about my view of women and society. She's extended the gift of updating her view of me. I used to be that college girl who wore Victorian boots and wanted nothing more than a husband and a brood of children. Now, married for eight years with one child on the way, I wear flip-flops and write and run a nonprofit with my husband. She's barely batted an eyelash as she's updated her understanding of who I've become.

Recently she relayed to me a frustrating experience in her new university job. Her superiors had disappointed her, leveraging their positions to line their pockets and shove their workload onto her shoulders. Tears filled her eyes as she said, "These are the people I've always looked up to, they have every reason to help others, they have good jobs. They're secure, but they're frauds."

As she kept talking I realized that she no longer felt sure that humans were basically good. I commiserated with her without mentioning that she was changing her mind about something we had debated in our college years. Instead of leaping to point out that her painful experience had significant spiritual meaning, I focused on updating my understanding of her beliefs.

Whenever we have a chance to witness a personal change, we consider it a privilege. Just like we want others to respond to our changes with acceptance, not accusing us or mocking us for our past views, we want to extend the same openness, allowing our friends to change their minds, including their ideas of spirituality.

Manner 6: Share Your Personal Experience

At the Monterey Aquarium, we were fascinated by the display of flower hat jellyfish. Each pane of glass gave us a peek into the gratuitous beauty of the undersea world. However, several sections of glass were smeared with small handprints. The smudged glass skewed our clear view of the creatures on the other side, so we relied on the information plaques beside each display.

But what if *all* the glass had been smudged and we only knew about jellyfish from reading the plaques, not from seeing them for ourselves? Our ability to communicate about the flower-hat jellies would be severely limited.

When we don't see Jesus, but merely rely on others' experience of him, sharing Jesus is more difficult and less clear to us and others.

When we don't see Jesus, but merely rely on others' experience of him, sharing Jesus is more difficult and less clear to us and others. We might be able to quote Bible verses or even follow a book's techniques for effective evangelism, but we will be underresourced for sharing the power of God in our lives.

Knowing how to talk about our experiences with Jesus will increase our ability to share him more than merely copying someone else's example. As we know him and as we enjoy his involvement in our lives, we will have more to naturally share with others.

We cannot share honestly what we do not know or understand. I (Dale) would never teach someone to flyfish a river unless I knew how myself. If I fake it, the day ends fishless and frustrating. Plus, the student dislikes the sport and doubts my competence.

It's easy to assume that simply because we call ourselves Christians, we also know how to talk about our life with Jesus. In reality, however, many of us don't know where to start or what to share. If we desire others to trust what we say, we need to know what we're talking about, not simply because we've heard others explain Jesus this way, but because we've experienced Jesus this way.

We can begin by thinking about our life with Jesus this last week. What have we noticed and loved about his involvement in our life? Can we share that?

I (Jonalyn) studied history because I once had a teacher who loved history. Likewise, if we can think of ways we enjoy Jesus, we can

Discipleship means we invite others into the life that we enjoy with Jesus.

more easily share our gladness for him. We can even make disciples. Discipleship means we invite others into the life that we enjoy with Jesus. As theologian and pastor R. A. Torrey published in a collection of essays, "One must know, experimentally, the power and joy of the Gospel before he is competent to tell it out."[4]

The good news always includes Jesus, but we adapt it based on who we meet. If I (Jonalyn) meet a woman who cannot have children, I share my experience of my first pregnancy that ended in a miscarriage. I talk about how Jesus comforted me. And if I (Dale) talk with someone who is frustrated with their parents, I bring up the story of how my parents divorced when I was six and how Jesus has been re-parenting me since.

Unless we are sharing what we have experienced, we run the risk of spreading propaganda—things that make for great PR, but don't have evidence to back them up. If we have never experienced Jesus comforting us during a time of intense grief, how can we assure a friend that Jesus can help them? Our claims will ring false unless we speak out of our experiences with our God

One day we opened our door to two Jehovah's Witnesses. We listened as they shared how many Jehovah's Witnesses stood up against Hitler's Nazi regime. They excitedly shared about their predecessors' courage in the face of persecution.

I (Jonalyn) told them how much I loved having Jesus with me in times of persecution too. They nodded. Then I said, "I love Jesus' ability to suffer with us. And when we suffer, we enter into his suffering—the fellowship of suffering that Paul talks about. When I'm in pain it's wonderful to know I'm not alone. Jesus is with me."

They both listened without comment. Neither word of agreement nor refutation fell from their lips. Surprised, I saw that neither knew what I was talking about. They had not experienced the personal comfort and fellowship of suffering with Jesus.

He is part of our conversation because we love him, not because we feel like we have to make him look good.

We believe Jesus is the best thing to happen to this planet; he is the reason we can enjoy our lives. He gives us companionship when we grieve. He is part of our conversation because we love him, not because we feel like we have to make him look good. Sharing personal experiences of life with Jesus remains our number-one recommendation to make genuine and natural spiritual small talk.

Manner 7: Allow Others to Remain Unconvinced

If we practice these manners we will slowly see ourselves in friendship with those we might formerly have feared and mistrusted. If we practice this seventh manner, we will not get to a point where we force others to change their minds. We will allow our friends to remain unconvinced.

Granted, we've worked hard to give people space, to step into their shoes, to give them respect. We long to know if anything we've said made a difference and often feel squirmy when our friends have graciously moved to another subject. We strain to swim upstream, back to the previous discussion, with new reasons they should change their minds.

Lately, we've been taking notes on what really makes people change their minds. We've started with ourselves. What is the psychology of our gestalt switches?

We rarely change our minds in the heat of discussion and usually need several opportunities to hear new ideas before we adapt a new position. When I (Jonalyn) began writing about gender, I felt certain that women belonged in the hierarchy below men. I believed God taught women to submit to men, and all the examples I had read or experienced bore testimony that God created women to help and men to lead. But as I wrote my first book about women and their souls, as I read Scripture, theology, psychology, and gender studies, I found women who led men well and enjoyed God's favor.[5] I began meeting women who were competent, God-honoring leaders. As I found Bible-believing Christians who were convinced God cared more about the ordered beauty of a partnership than the order of hierarchy, I noticed that my views

> *New ideas change us slowly, like water on a rock, imperceptibly reshaping grooves and contours.*

were shifting. No one argued me into a new position — and had they tried to, at the beginning of my studies, it would likely have entrenched my hierarchical views more firmly! The change came slowly, taking nearly three years of intense study, praying, writing, and questioning.

New ideas change us slowly, like water on a rock, imperceptibly reshaping grooves and contours. Slow change requires space within friendships, time for reflection, and consistent relationship that allows these ideas to surface again and again.

When I (Dale) was in sixth grade, a man came to our church to teach us "soul-winning." He gave away Bibles, pre-underlined and pre-noted for sharing our faith. I tried the technique on my friend, Max.

In my bedroom, I pulled out the little Bible and showed Max some verses. I thought the Bible verses would magically convict and convert him. Although disinterested, Max finally agreed to listen like a real friend when I insisted I had to go through the program of verses with him. I invited him to pray, but he said he'd do it later — he wanted to go play outside. *I can't leave him to think on his own,* I thought. *He might die tonight!*

The opportunity was now or never, so I leveraged our play with conversion. "We cannot go out to play until you say this prayer." Max bowed his head and repeated the prayer that I read. Abusing our friendship was worth it if I could ensure he left my room with a passport to heaven.

We stuck together into our teens as we turned into punks.[6] I wonder what turn our friendship would have taken had I not been so insistent. Would he have become a better influence on me when I struggled? Would he later have found a way to let Jesus help him and in turn let Jesus help me? I will never know.

When I (Jonalyn) studied in London, I befriended Heather. I was so eager to introduce her to Jesus that I regularly gave her reasons for accepting Christianity. Within a few months, she accepted Christ and started coming to church with me. But upon returning home, our friendship fizzled. She stopped coming to church. I never saw her. It was then that I realized we had not cultivated a friendship outside of my efforts to convert her. I didn't consider until too late that I had pressured her to accept Jesus almost as a condition to continue our friendship. I don't think I considered it worthwhile leaving Heather unconvinced. I thought making the most of the opportunity meant maintaining pressure on her to accept Jesus. We don't talk anymore.

But Annie, my other close friend from the London trip, would listen to my arguments for the Bible and then debate them. I remember I liked her company but was constantly feeling derailed from my witnessing plan. Annie would never let me finish. After thirty minutes of debating some biblical idea back and forth, Annie would invariably smile and gently change the subject to our common interests. We had plenty we could agree on—art, drama, good writing. Eventually, I learned that I enjoyed talking with her more when I let her remain unconvinced. Annie taught me how to enjoy a friendship without pressuring someone to agree. I believe this is why we remain friends today.

Avoiding that itch for closure and focusing on the person before us means we're living out Jesus' patient love. What does my friend want to talk about? Am I sensitive to respecting *their* freedom to be unconvinced by my points? Whenever a spiritual topic is changed—even by something as innocuous as the server appearing with our plate of food—we can use the pause to gauge how demanding we've become about our topic. Are we willing to relinquish conversational control?

Avoiding that itch for closure and focusing on the person before us means we're living out Jesus' patient love.

Leaving a topic for another time and parting with grace proves our conviction that God is wiser and more persuasive than we, better at softening the human heart in his timing. Paradoxically, this allows us to bring up the topic again more easily, since our friends see we won't hold onto our God-topic obnoxiously. Instead, they will see someone who loves without making demands.

These conversational manners help us gather friends for our journey. And we've learned that the more we walk with Jesus, the less we have to think about the manners. These manners will become part of lives, where we know them and naturally live by them in love. Yet every conversation has its risks, and despite our best efforts, conversation stoppers pop up all too often.

Chapter 3

Conversation Stoppers

The summer before my senior year in high school, I (Jonalyn) left my small Christian school of 500 students, moved by the desire to see God change my local public school through me. La Serna High School boasted 2,000 students, an Olympic-sized pool, and plenty of shocking behavior (at least to my sheltered eyes). I lost no time scouting out missionary opportunities.

In AP English I sat next to Paul, a tall, brown-haired athlete. One morning while we were supposed to be discussing Rousseau, he said he was an atheist. I was ready to pounce with some apologetic tools. "How can you be totally sure God isn't there? You can't be everywhere at once looking for him."

He already looked nervous, but I continued, "So I think you're probably an agnostic; because it's impossible to be certain there is no God."

"Fine, I'm agnostic." He didn't look pleased with my helpfulness.

"So how do you think the universe got here?" I pressed.

"I think, I mean, it makes sense to me that ..." He uncomfortably finished with, "I believe, uh, that evolution is true." His voice inflected up, as if he was asking me whether that answer would suffice. At that word, every witnessing tool came out, sharpened and gleaming.

"You *do?*" Sarcasm dripped from my voice, "You actually believe evolution is *true?!* The world just popped into existence? It just *happened?*" I might have well have said, "You are an idiot!"

Paul picked up what I was putting down. His tentative side disappeared and out came the jock personality. The rest of the year, our interactions were limited to his teasing my strict prim and proper personality and my attempts to defend myself. In retrospect, I don't blame him. I had just killed our conversational potential.

No matter our personality and educational level, we can destroy opportunities for conversation. We raise topics better left unsaid. We state our opinion unasked. We get facts wrong. We insult, we look shocked or disgusted—and the spiritual small talk screeches to a halt.

Let us tell you straightaway: both of us have made the gospel look ridiculous or paltry, either with our words or our actions. Yet Jesus still uses us, and we're learning as we go. God's work is not dependent on our "success"—God isn't nervously watching from heaven, hoping we don't get it wrong. Instead, God invites us to grow, learning as we go and showing us ways to be ready to love better. We want to share some of our mistakes so that you'll be able to avoid the following conversation stoppers in your friendships.

> *God isn't nervously watching from heaven, hoping we don't get it wrong.*

"Just Take It by Faith"

Lara, a new Christian, was training two new ski instructors. During their lunch break, the older of the two, Veronika, brought up a question about Jesus.

"How do you know Jesus wasn't African?" she asked Lara. "Doesn't the Bible say something like Jesus was from Egypt?"

Lara's eyes descended on her sandwich. How should she respond? She took another bite to buy some time. Veronika's co-worker chimed in, "Well, in all the paintings I've seen, Jesus is white!"

"He couldn't be white!" Veronika said. "Everyone thinks Jesus is their ethnicity! He wasn't from Europe, that's for sure!" Then they turned to Lara for the Christian answer.

Lara piped in, complimenting them both. "It's so good to discuss religion. There's a lot of mystery in Christianity. If you understood everything, then you'd have science, and religion is not science. You just have to take some things by faith."

Many of us are tempted to use spiritual words to get out of feeling cornered.

The two co-workers went back to their argument. When they heard "faith," they heard "believing something without evidence." Lara undercut her credibility, unintentionally punting the argument out of the world of facts into personal opinion or "faith." Instead of admitting she didn't know, she solidified what many believe about Christians—we are not as interested in truth as we are in our faith.

However, Lara left her lunch break positive this conversation gave her a chance to point to the centrality of faith in her religion. Lara didn't mean to reduce Jesus to a matter of personal opinion.

Like Lara, many of us are tempted to use spiritual words to get out of feeling cornered. Instead of pondering a question or honestly admitting we don't know, we stop the conversation with a confusing reply.

"Just take it by faith" kills conversations. The idiom distorts the biblical understanding of the word *faith*. (For more on the Bible's view of faith, flip to page 101.) Today, most people think of faith as a blind, irrational leap. Listen to Elizabeth Gilbert explain faith in *Eat, Pray, Love*: "If faith were rational, it wouldn't be—by definition—faith. Faith is walking face-first and full-speed into the dark."[1] Gilbert, who doesn't consider herself a Christian, thinks faith opposes reason. Sadly, so do many Christians. The skeptic's dictionary defines faith as "a non-rational belief in some proposition."[2] Atheists and skeptics use this antibiblical definition of faith to mock Christians as idiots.

If we are going to share the good news of Jesus with others, we need to make a point to avoid the phrase, "Just take it by faith." We're inadvertently telling our friends that Jesus is not real enough to know and that we cannot share reasons to believe in him.

"That's the Way I Was Raised"

In the 2009 Miss USA pageant, Miss California, Carrie Prejean, responded to a question about legalizing same-sex marriage. Prejean told judges her honest view; she believed marriage should be between a man and a woman. That may have been a courageous response, given the setting, but she supplied a poor reason, saying, "That's the way I was raised."

We often hear a similar response in open forums when speaking to students about different religions. A Hindu, Christian, or Muslim may announce their upbringing as their number-one reason to believe their religion: "I was raised that way." While this may be true of their upbringing, as students grow into adulthood, they need to each study and discover other reasons for their faith beyond their parents' convictions. I (Dale) heard something similar in my Christian college years. Pastors recommended the King James Version of the Bible not with historical evidence, but with statements like, "If the King James was good enough for my grandfather, it's good enough for me."

Our upbringing should not be the single reason we, as adults, subscribe to a political or religious view. However godly our ancestors, our views do not become right or wrong simply because we follow in their footsteps. No son of a slave trader would get away with that excuse.

Showing Fear or Hatred

When one of our three dogs was a puppy, she frequently attacked the other dogs. During meals or playtimes, Lady Jane would growl or bite. We soon discovered that she suffered from fear, not rage — her anxiety and whimpering increased whenever we pet and praised the other dogs. But when we pet her and spoke kindly to her, she became our most affectionate, obedient corgi.

Often we lash out at others because we feel threatened. We don't particularly want to hurt them, but we fear that what they stand for might threaten us or the things we value.

Frederick Buechner, reflecting on the words of John, says that while "perfect love casts out fear ... fear casts out love, even God's love."[3] We don't lash out when we feel safe. But when we are fearful, we often, without thinking, go on the attack. We need to double-check what's going on in our souls and ask ourselves why we're choking out love. Do we fear we won't get what we need for ourselves, for our families, for our future? Are we like Lady Jane, feeling anxious that we're being overlooked? Or are we moving toward others with love, concern, and a desire to know them?

We fear that what they stand for might threaten us or the things we value.

There is a fine line between fear and hatred. Sometimes we're only acting out of fear, but we appear to others as hateful.

I (Jonalyn) shared previously about my friend from junior high who is now a lesbian (page 38). She told me about the way certain Christians' fear looked like hatred to her. She told me of Fred Phelps, the man who claims to be a Christian but who holds signs that read "God hates fags!" at public events. Phelps says God wants him to spread the message that God does not love everyone. My friend told me the only way she knows to cope with his hatred: "I made a pact with God. I share who I am, honestly, and God takes care of my heart."

In our conversation, she echoed Beuchner's words, "The opposite of love is not hate, but fear." In one of her emails she wrote:

It was terribly hard to come out. Growing up in the church hearing homosexuality was the ultimate sin and that God would not love me was terrible. I didn't understand a hateful God. I lived my life the best way I knew how and did the best I could. I went away from the church for a long time. I felt shameful, hurt, abused, and distant, and that is not what Jesus or the God I knew would want me to feel.

When I came out to my Christian friends, I was met with "but you will go to hell" and other such nice things. When you hear that enough, you will turn away from anyone. Who deserves to hear that? I didn't choose this life ... I didn't *choose* to be gay. I prayed from the time when we were at junior high together until about age twenty-one for God to take these feelings away from me. I immersed myself in the church, Bible studies, Christian camps, all hoping that by doing that, he would make me "normal." What I realized is that I am normal.

I really try to be calm and patient with people who say I can't love God because I am gay. That is just atrocious. I believe God made me who I am for a reason, and my sole purpose in life is to follow the teachings of Jesus and love all ... to not judge others ... I follow in the life of someone who loved no matter what.[4]

Do we require people to "clean up" before we invite them into our homes and lives? Does our fear lead us to hate the sin and the sinner too?

Showing Disgust

Disgust chokes our love as well. If we see a few homeless people and our inner monologue goes something like — *Probably addicted to alcohol, sleeping on the streets because of poor choices. That's what happens. He's an addict — and smells horrible!* — then we cannot love our neighbor. Our disgust prevents us from seeing them as human. We don't want to touch them, let alone affirm and love them.

Jesus never found other people disgusting or shocking, no matter how depraved or dirty or chaotic. The more we grow to be unshockable, like Jesus, the closer we are to being Jesus to others.

Not long ago Jonalyn and I were leaving a National Pastor's Convention in San Diego when we spotted a large man holding a sign begging for food. Driving past would have been easy, but we had heard Shane Claiborne talk that weekend about being Jesus

Jesus never found other people disgusting or shocking, no matter how depraved or dirty or chaotic.

to the hungry. Jonalyn suggested that we buy a hot meal for the homeless man.

I was unconvinced. My disgust germinated against this homeless man, not for being homeless, but for taking advantage of others and refusing to contribute to society. *This high-traffic intersection offers enough opportunity*, I thought. *He probably gets plenty.*

However, Jonalyn insisted we buy a *warm* meal, so we ordered a burrito full of veggies and carried it across four lanes of traffic to the tall, homeless man. He lowered his sign and his eyes lit up. "Oh, thank you!" he beamed, wrinkling his chin, his voice cracking, "I haven't eaten all day!"

"What's your name?" Jonalyn asked. As we talked with him, I felt cruel for my disgust and prejudice. Jonalyn asked Jesus to bless him before we left.

"God bless you both," he replied. He turned back to his shopping cart, tucked in his sign, sat down, and relaxed with a mouthful of burrito.

Jonalyn has lots of stories of helping the homeless. In each one, she ends up helped by them, often moved to tears by their plight. "Dale, he was so *hungry!*" she'll tell me. I'm learning to overcome my disgust, not by wishing to be nicer, but by intentionally interacting with people I don't understand, people who are easy to dismiss or discount.

Sin Sniffing

Christians sometimes act like cops, pulling people aside for breaking a biblical rule. Our psychologist friend, Dr. Ellen Quarry, once sat with a boy who had just tattled on his friend. "With every person we meet, we can choose to be a cop or an angel. Maybe your friend doesn't need you to tell on him every time he does something wrong. Maybe he just needs you to ask him to play with you."

Sin sniffing comes easily, especially in the moral areas we think we've mastered. We reveal our sin-sniffing noses when we internally rejoice when our enemy stumbles or when we say their sin is "what we expected all along."

Rules are helpful training wheels, but God calls us to something that is both more difficult and more enjoyable. I (Dale) grew up in an environment of religious addiction.[5] I followed the rules because I felt a sense of satisfaction with my accomplishment. I felt safe that no one would catch me, blame me, or exclude me from the group. My family faithfully attended church three times a week. Mom sang in the choir. My sister and I joined youth group. Even on vacation, we felt guilty if we didn't hunt down a place of worship on Sunday morning. Why did I feel like a bad person for disliking youth group meetings? Why did I think that all guilty feelings were from God?

They live as cops because they believe God is more "cop" than "angel," and they're trying to be like their God.

In my mid-teens I learned that I could ask questions without inciting divine wrath. I learned that God would walk with me and help me answer and live with my questions.[6] Many people, regardless of religion, have never felt free to let God love them. They live as cops because they believe God is more "cop" than "angel," and they're trying to be like their God.

In my twenties, my mother began to uncover the sin-sniffing attitude in those around her as she asked her own questions while she battled cancer. She started identifying ways we manipulate one another, using blaming and shaming words to motivate good behavior. She taught me that Jesus wanted shame-free followers, apprentices who knew that guilt was not a destination.

Shaming and blaming works well to whip ourselves into shape, but it inaccurately teaches us that our worth is linked to our good behavior. Since we all long to feel worthy, we all try to behave. And we shame-and-blame ourselves and others we're trying to talk to about Jesus.

Shaming or blaming has tempted many parents as an effective child-rearing method. If a mother catches her nine-year-old son stealing a handful of newly baked cookies and reprimands him, "Didn't I train you better than that? Those are for the party," she's communicating, "Aren't you smart enough to see I was saving those?" Without lifting her hand to swat him, her words hurt him worse than a spanking. The boy, psychologically beaten into obedience, will likely never steal a cookie again, because stealing makes him less worthy, less smart, less loved.

At another level, but in more subtle form, Christians are often guilty of drumming up volunteers for church programs with shaming questions like, "If you don't pray for a teen, who will?" or, "Isn't the children's ministry important to you?" or, "How can you expect God to bless you if you don't tithe to the church?" These questions subtly ask, "Don't you know good Christians help out with the nursery?" or, "Tithing proves you are growing in your faith; you do want to grow, right?"[a] Shaming often uses half-true ideas to manipulate people to do what we think God wants. Shaming leverages our approval in a relationship to get people to do the "godly" thing. In the end those who capitulate have not really chosen freely because they chose out of fear of disapproval more than their desire to help. Shaming and blaming works. As long as someone fears their commitment to Christ will be questioned without regular volunteering at their church, we will always have eager volunteers. But these methods do not compel real love nor make our souls like Jesus. We're motivating others to do good, not because they love the teens or toddlers or the church, but because they fear losing acceptance in the community's eyes. Just like the child who abstains from stealing, not

As long as someone fears their commitment to Christ will be questioned without regular volunteering at their church, we will always have eager volunteers.

------

[a] See "spiritual abuse" on page 191.

because he knows stealing a cookie is wrong, but because he's afraid he will lose his mother's love.

When my (Jonalyn's) teenage friend found out she was pregnant, her youth pastor approached me and said, "How is your friend handling all this?" I told him that it was difficult, but it seemed like she would be okay.

He responded with words I'll never forget: "With that kind of mistake, I don't think she's going to be okay." He killed the conversation. Without regard for the natural consequences of sin, he felt that he had to emphasize her shame.

If we have been raised with shame or blame, we no longer need others to blame and shame us. We will believe we're worthless human beings, and we will accept abuses from others as somehow being our fault. Shame and blame teaches us that we are unworthy of love and builds a wall separating us from God's love. We can tell if we're a shamer or blamer by how often the word *should* comes up in our self-talk. Do we use "good" behavior like regular devotions, church attendance, and prayer to keep our guilty feelings at bay?

> *We will believe we're worthless human beings, and we will accept abuses from others as somehow being our fault.*

Sin sniffing spills out in our demeanor, in our perspectives, and in our conversations. If we see this tendency in ourselves, we can be sure others see it leaking from us too. Our friends will think of our God as a sin sniffer, as a blamer and shamer. Our guilt-ridden statements will end our spiritual conversations and skew what Jesus' life looks like in us. Yet Jesus, again, shows us a way forward.

Being a moral person is not necessarily the same as walking in Jesus' freedom. Look again at Jesus kneeling down to help the paralytic or the prostitute. His gentle but authoritative power resounds like a symphony, "Your sins are forgiven!" He doesn't tell them to grovel or beat themselves up. He doesn't ask them to prove how sorry they are or to volunteer at the local synagogue. Often he doesn't even point out their sins. Instead, he asks them what they seek and invites them into new life. The paralytic responds with tears of joy and dancing.[7]

Jesus with the paralytic offers us a picture more accurate than any cop or sin-sniffing old man in the heavens.[8] We need this picture of freely offered love. Our neighbor needs the same picture from us. The next time we catch ourselves saying, "You need to try harder," let's allow our failure to serve as a reminder that in Jesus' kingdom, failure points to our need for Jesus, not to our worthlessness. In the kingdom of God, repentance is a response to forgiveness, not a prerequisite for forgiveness.[9]

In Jesus' kingdom, failure points to our need for Jesus, not to our worthlessness.

Nothing disconnects people from Jesus more quickly than us teaching them they are shameful or worthless for being sinners, which often comes through in our Christian-talk of being "unworthy" or "worms" in the eyes of God. After speaking at a Christian high school, a sophomore came up to me (Dale) and said, "We always get speakers telling us how we're sinners. Thank you for treating us like we want to grow and not beating us up. I liked how you talked about why we're valuable." While we may not merit God's love, this is different from being a worthless creature. We want to be careful that our words are accurate.

God doesn't play the shame-and-blame game with us. Genesis 1–2 teaches that each of us splashes God's image of earth. Maybe you need a refresher in how Jesus really treated the sinners.[10] Ask God to help you see others—and yourself—through the eyes of Jesus: as reflections of a God whose loving-kindness never ceases.[b]

---

[b] Lamentations 3:22.

Chapter 4

Jesus: The Way, the Truth, and the Good Life

Jesus told a story about a man with fine taste. A collector-dealer of precious jewels regularly bought fine pearls. One day he found a pearl so flawless and rare that he took immediate action: he gathered up his entire collection of gems — his life's work — and sold every one at the market, much to the enthusiasm of competing jewelry merchants. With his pockets full of cash, he returned to that flawless, rare pearl and purchased it.[1]

Jesus and his students assumed the rare pearl was worth the trade. No one raised their hand in protest at the ignorance of the pearl collector. He was the expert who knew the value was worth the sacrifice.

Jesus told this story to highlight what the kingdom of heaven is like. The kingdom makes us willing to give all our stored-up treasures. Jesus wasn't speaking about "heaven" as some destination in the sky for us after we die. Jesus' kingdom of heaven is God's movement, God's work, God's rule over the universe in the present. The merchant sold all he had because he wanted to wrap his destiny into reality, a kingdom where God will bring all things to their good and proper end. This same kingdom is now available to us, where God is at the center, slowly but steadfastly orchestrating an overarching peace between ethnicities, genders, nations, socioeconomic and age groups. God's kingdom, his literal reign over all the nations, makes us all more human. The merchant sold all he had because he wanted to be part of God bringing all those things we hunger for: justice, love, rest, community, and delight.

Each of us longs to find the one thing that is worth our entire life. When we find it, we are willing to give up everything to hold on to it.

Each of us longs to find the one thing that is worth our entire life.

Every religion in the world, even many crafted by spiritual designers, asks a price for its pearl. A Buddhist gives up her desires in order to end her suffering. A Hindu who follows Kali, the goddess of destruction, may give up the best fruits and incense at the temple in worship. A spiritual designer may give up the evening news or certain food in order to keep his body and soul pure.

We know that good things are worthy of sacrifice. Yet, today, we're not convinced religion deserves all that much sacrifice. As Eugene Peterson says, "People often see spirituality as outside of real human life."[2] Many people see spirituality as an add-on for those blessed with the luxury to pursue spiritual things. Yet Jesus connects spirituality to every gritty aspect of life.

A Dehumanizing Spirituality

A test of the authenticity of any view is whether it allows us to use all our human capacities. A spiritual designer, Rocky, and his Buddhist friend, Barry, joined us last summer for dinner.[3] Knowing that Rocky was a vegetarian, we roasted up some vegetables and served them with pasta. While we watched the sunset, the conversation moved from organic food to hearing their story of a recent ecstatic experience at a Hindu temple. They both called themselves "seekers of truth."

Then Rocky wanted to hear how we experienced God. I (Jonalyn) shared how I experienced freedom in God through the story of my parking-lot meltdown (read it here on page 28). Dale talked about his suffering through spiritual abuse and leaning on Jesus' strength. They loved hearing about our experiences. As we grew more comfortable discussing spirituality, our questions deepened, and I piped up. "Rocky, I keep hearing you say that God is love and that love is God. But when you say 'God,' do you mean God is a person who gives love and receives love, or do you mean God is a love force that we can harness?"

A test of the authenticity of any view is whether it allows us to use all our human capacities.

Rocky responded, "God is infinite, and we can never describe God. We can only experience him."

Dale replied, "But infinite doesn't mean we can't know *anything*, only that we'll never know *everything*, right? God can be infinite, but we can still know some things about God, like you just said, you know God can be experienced. That's something to know."

Barry joined in at this point: "When people think of God like a person, you get problems. A God in our image ... he's just like the God of the Greeks—Zeus. He can have likes and dislikes; we can use him and control him."

I challenged him on that point: "What if the exact opposite is true, that *we* are made in *God's* image? What if thinking of God without personality makes God safer and easier to control? Manipulating an inanimate object like a chair is much easier than controlling and relating to a personal God."

Rocky took the classic Buddhist line. He warned us about using our reason. "Reason gets in the way—it clouds the path."

I thought he might be referencing the Buddhist Eightfold Path, so I asked him what Buddha's "Right Intention" and "Right Mindfulness" meant, if not to use our reason to understand.[4]

He responded, "The right mindfulness means to be *in* every moment, not the past, not the future. Your mind is a tool to realize the unity of us all, not to focus on minutiae."

"Are you saying I can't rely on my reason to think about the world?" I waved my hand toward the mountains around the valley. Barry and Rocky nodded, like we were finally getting it.

Dale asked, "Then why would we find ourselves in this world with the human tool of reason if we're not supposed to use it? Why do we have this ability to think about the world if we're supposed to deny it?"

"Our feelings can be trusted, but not our reason." To us, Barry seemed to be using reason to come to this conclusion. But Dale did not challenge him about this; instead he brought up our humanity.

"I want to use my reason because it seems to be an important part of being human. I want a religion that asks me to test it with my reason, not to put it aside," Dale explained. "We want to follow the religion that helps us be not merely spiritual, but appropriately human."

They both looked at us, the idea dawning on them as if for the first time. They both slowly nodded at us. Rocky said, "You know, that makes sense."

The Human Way of Jesus

By coming to earth in the flesh, Jesus put his stamp of approval on what humans are. Jesus' life proves God still finds humans worth redeeming. Therefore, we should be hesitant to sell everything and buy into a religion or any spiritual pearl of great price if it invalidates any of our human tools. Denying reason, ignoring intuition, or dismissing emotional intelligence might prevent us from choosing wisely. Why would we risk any spiritual path without bringing all our tools to the project?

We should be hesitant to sell everything and buy into a religion or any spiritual pearl of great price if it invalidates any of our human tools.

God has gifted us with many ways to detect spiritual truth: imagination, intuition, emotion, perception, experience, and community to name a few. Any religion or spirituality that disregards one or more of our abilities is likely to make us less, not more, human and thereby less like Jesus. As philosopher Dallas Willard writes, "The correct perspective is to see following Christ not only as the necessity it is, but as the fulfillment of the highest human possibilities and as life on the highest plane.[5]

The Point of Truth

Sometimes we've been tempted to defend the truth at all costs, as if truth, by itself, trumps everything else in the world. Apologists emphasize that we, as Christians, have the truth. We have apologetic series like Focus on the Family's "The Truth Project" and books like Nancy Pearcey's *Total Truth*. All these campaigns and books offer helpful ways to understand the world. Truth is always helpful as it always guides our lives.

But our evangelical assumptions and conversations tend to start and end with the truth. While truth gives us principles to live by, life is more than having the facts right. Truth is part of life but not the totality of life. Truth isn't our home, but truth guides us home.

Truth isn't our home, but truth guides us home.

One autumn we visited Moab, Utah, for a Jeep adventure. The sun sank in a clear sky. We chose a casual, moderate trail ride in the twilight. As we bumped along, we had no idea that flash floods had washed out the trail a week earlier.

Guided only by our headlights, we crisscrossed streams, following the trail signs over boulders and around brush. In places, the trail was narrow and difficult, the trail's edges disappearing into dark ravines. Turning around was nearly impossible. Hours rolled past as we straddled ruts and hugged cliffs.

Time after time we lost the trail, but when we thought we were truly lost, we'd spot a smudged set of wide Jeep tracks left in the mud, pointing the way forward. If that driver made it through the washouts, we could too.

Hours after midnight, we finished at the highway, where we danced to U2's "Beautiful Day" blasting from the stereo, grateful for the tracks that led us home.

Truth, like those tracks, leads us through the wilderness and safely onto the other side. But we didn't dance for the tracks. We danced because we were still alive, that we made it out. Yet, by the way some followers of Jesus talk, in our apologetics or in our churches, truth is the whole show; the tracks on the trail are the entire point.

Truth, like those tracks, leads us through the wilderness and safely onto the other side.

Too often we assume that evidence for truth will compel people to agree, to convert, to side with us. But others may only see us pointing to tracks in the mud when we haven't told them how these tracks lead them somewhere. Most people don't want truth for its own sake; they only want truth if it leads them to a place they've been looking for. But where are the tracks going? Why should I follow your Jesus over his Buddha? Will this path guide me to the place that will satisfy my deepest longings? Will it get me there in one piece, validating all my human experience and all my human faculties? Is it worth me selling everything I have to purchase this pearl of great price?

Jesus emphasized the significance of our destination when he gave his famous line, "You will know the truth, and the truth will set you free."[a] After we spoke at a large, affluent school, one teenager wrote us:

> What touched me was when you said "the truth will set you free," and right then I totally started crying, which I never do. I've never heard that before. My dad says the point of life is to live and die without fear, but after you guys talked, I totally changed my mind. I feel pretty strongly about Christianity and finally being able to believe it as truth.

For her, truth ceased to be a track in the mud but a means to a life she wanted. She discovered that truth connected her life with freedom; truth pointed her down the path to a good life.

---

[a] John 8:32.

The Good Life

Many people bullied by truth—or rather by *people* who abuse truth—are turned off by the very term. Christians sharing Jesus' exclusive truth claims get labeled fanatical or pushy or close-minded. But if we want to show others the face of Jesus, we can turn to more reasons beyond truth that Jesus gave for following him.

What other ways does Jesus talk about himself?

Jesus used images to indicate that he is the center of every human story. When he called himself the *light of the world*, he meant that he shines a light into every part of our lives. Jesus also offered himself as the *bread of life*, alluding to the God of Israel sustaining the Jewish people through the wilderness. The sustenance that the manna from heaven gave the Jews is now made flesh and offered to every person on earth. "For the bread of God is the bread that comes down from heaven and gives life to the world ... I am the living bread that comes down from heaven."[b] Jesus told the Samaritan woman at the well that he could give *living water*; the life he offered was qualitatively better. "Those who drink the water I give them will never thirst. Indeed, the water I give them will become in them a spring of water welling up to eternal life." Eternal life begins

> *Jesus lets us experience all those things every human being longs for—love, joy, peace—the many fruits of his Spirit in Galatians.*

when we know Jesus here on this earth, not when we enter heaven after death. The good life of God springs up in us now, like water in our bodies, replenishing our world-weary souls.

Perhaps out of fear that we're falsely advertising Jesus' way as an easy way to get all our pleasures fulfilled, we avoid sharing these biblical offers. But if Jesus devoted himself to these pictures of the good life, we can pass them on.

When we share Jesus as "the life," we want others to see how without Jesus we cannot fulfill our fullest human potential. Jesus

---

[b] John 6:33, 51.

lets us experience all those things every human being longs for—love, joy, peace—the many fruits of his Spirit in Galatians.ᶜ Without Jesus, our lives are not abundant. As philosopher and spiritual director Dallas Willard explains:

> Nondiscipleship costs abiding peace, a life penetrated throughout by love, faith that sees everything in the light of God's overriding governance for good, hopefulness that stands firm in the most discouraging of circumstances, power to do what is right and withstand the forces of evil. In short, it costs exactly that abundant life Jesus said he came to bring. The cross-shaped yoke of Christ is after all an instrument of liberation and power to those who live in it with him and learn the meekness and lowliness of heart that brings rest to the soul.[6]

If Jesus offers so much, why do we have such a hard time explaining him to others? In the next section, we'll take a fresh look at how to read the Bible, how to use common "lost words" such as *sin* and *love*, and how to approach other religions. Come along with us as we restock our tools to share how Jesus gives light to this world.

ᶜ Galatians 5:22–23.

Part II

Restocking Your Tools

Chapter 5

How to Read the Bible

After speaking in a New England church, one woman echoed a popular, though hidden, sentiment: "The more I read the Bible, the more my doubts grow. I've stopped reading in order to hold on to my faith." Perhaps you feel the same way, wondering about difficult passages, sticking to clear sections to keep from doubting. Have you felt worried that a skeptical person might ask you to explain something in the Bible that you haven't figured out either?

A young man in Arizona felt that apologetic books did not help him answer some of his deeper questions about the Bible itself. One of the nagging thoughts he had, as he saw Scripture quoted, was the way different preachers found "deeper meanings" in the Bible, meanings he could never have discovered. He started to doubt that the Bible had any objective meaning. Many Christians were using the Bible to sanction multiple, sometimes contradictory ideas.

Years into his search, I (Dale) met him at a multiday apologetics event, where he quietly attended every evening, sitting in the second row. Throughout the week I spoke on the existence of God, the limits of science, the historical reliability of Scripture, and the resurrection of Jesus—staple apologetic topics. The last evening, I changed gears and taught how to read the Bible intelligently. Afterward, the young man shook my hand and said, "Of all the talks this week, this one helped me the most!"

Many begin a journey away from Christianity and into spiritual designing because the Bible feels wooden, difficult to understand, and unfit for contemporary life.

For all the love Christians claim for the Bible, we find many baffled by this book. Many rely on pastors and popular Bible studies more than on their knowledge of how to clearly and confidently look up a passage and explain what it means. We've discovered that unless you know how to read and interpret the Bible, defending it as God's Word may not be all that helpful. Anyone can easily pull out a stumping question. If we're confused about what the Bible means, we'll feel inadequate to explain and defend it.

Many rely on pastors and popular Bible studies more than on their knowledge of how to clearly and confidently look up a passage and explain what it means.

Since God's Word is a tether to our Father's heart, our main resource for human flourishing, a privilege of correspondence inspired by God, we give others hope and clarity when we show them we understand the Bible. We believe the Bible is inspired, meaning that God, the Holy Spirit, influenced men to pen an accurate record of what God intended for us to read and know.[1] With all the seekers in this world dabbling in religion and spiritual experience, we can reintroduce the Scriptures to them and refresh our own confidence that the Bible makes sense.

Abusing the Bible

Christians often treat the Bible like an inspirational quotation book or a magical source of power. We grab verses out of context and stick them on magnets or bumper stickers. We force a biblical passage to fit our situation, rarely pausing to note the authors' intentions to lift us into a story larger than our own.

Misusing the Bible means people don't hear what God originally wrote. Misusing Scripture hides the original meaning of God's Word as much as assuming the Bible is full of errors. Both are equally damaging as they keep people from trusting the Bible as a source of truth.

We've misused the Bible to make ourselves look better, like quoting, "Judge not lest you be judged" to deflect criticism from our view.[a] If we quote Hebrews, "Do not forsake the assembling together" to enforce regular attendance at the church building, we're also misusing the Bible. If we use David slaying Goliath as a story for tips on how to take out the giant problems in our own lives, we're misusing the Bible. We may be sharing good ideas, but we miss the truth that the author intended.

Misusing Scripture hides the original meaning of God's Word as much as assuming the Bible is full of errors.

Even the most brilliant, historical minds were caught misusing the Bible at times, like Augustine in the 400s, who often read portions of the Bible as pure allegory. He allegorized the Good Samaritan story by interpreting the beaten man as Adam, the Good Samaritan as Jesus, the oil as comfort of good hope, the wine as exhortation to work with a fervent spirit, the donkey as the flesh of Christ's incarnation, the inn as the church, and the innkeeper as Paul.[2] In the process he missed the point Jesus was making — a story explaining how every human, including the social outcast, is our neighbor. In the 1800s, Christians in the South used Canaan's curse to defend slavery. Today, many skeptics wonder what other hurtful views we hold because we've found Bible verses to back us up. They cannot take the Bible seriously when we quote Scripture to both defend and decry the death penalty, to enforce patriarchy and to liberate women, to justify capitalism and promote socialism.

Our intent isn't to discourage you but instead to help you weigh the importance and potential divisions our various interpretations make. We want to put the same tools into everyone's hands and see what unity and humility we can build together.

Rather than quoting selective verses to "get someone saved," or avoiding the Bible completely because we're afraid we can't interpret

---

[a] Luke 6:37; Matt. 7:1-2.

it, we can all better prepare ourselves to share our faith by knowing how to read our Bibles. The most helpful book we've found today is *How to Read the Bible for All Its Worth* by Gordon D. Fee and Douglas Stuart, which offers a straightforward introduction on how to read and apply Scripture. Many of their ideas are sprinkled throughout this chapter.

Lucky Dipping

The words of Isaiah wrapped around the walls of my (Jonalyn's) junior high locker room. Words penned 3,000 years ago reassured me and my fellow athletes that God would give us energy. "They will mount up with wings like eagles ... they will run and not be faint."[b] As a track runner, I believed God promised me stamina on the last lap of my 2400-meter race.

I never doubted those words applied directly to me, a teenager in the twentieth century. Isaiah fit my life in that moment, so I grabbed hold. Besides, our adult coach had stapled them up for us; she would know if they applied to us. Those words pushed me, churning through my mind while I ran. Wasn't the Bible supposed to inspire us? How could it be wrong to take a verse out of context if I sensed God speaking to me through it?

How could it be wrong to take a verse out of context if I sensed God speaking to me through it?

I had no idea of the original audience or context. It was enough that God put it into the Bible. I had, unwittingly, begun to practice lucky dipping.

How could it be wrong to take a verse out of context if I sensed God speaking to me through it?

Many Christians dip into their Bibles with hopes to find a bit of comfort and courage. Anyone can "lucky dip" in any book. We have friends who lucky dip into the Qur'an, into tarot cards, into

---

[b] Isaiah 40:31.

Jane Austen's novels, or into Christian devotionals. We're tempted to lucky dip anytime we approach the Bible for a quick fix.

I remember from my Christian school teaching days how lucky dipping tempted many teachers to use the following plan: (1) write up a lesson; (2) look up key words in a biblical concordance; and (3) cut and paste select verses into lesson.

Lucky dipping into the Bible could make us do horrible things. The classic joke is opening to Matthew 27:5 that says Judas "went away and hanged himself," closing your Bible, and then opening to John 13:27, "What you are about to do, do quickly." Apparently, a speedy suicide is commanded in Scripture.

Perhaps this sounds too outlandish. But Christians have developed a reputation for taking verses at random and applying them to their lives. We're tempted to lucky dip by the merchandise sold to us, "Testamints" that include a short Bible verse along with a breath mint and Christian books that insert a fragmented Bible verse at the beginning of each chapter. Selective snippets of Scripture on mugs, cross-stitch, T-shirts, and jewelry boxes encourage us to misapply God's words, unless we know the real meaning. Often we do not. Theologian Miroslav Volf calls this selective fragmentation of Scripture a symptom of "thin religion" full of zeal but not "rely[ing] on a full understanding of the sacred writings of Scripture."[3]

> *God* intended *what's in the Bible, not whatever we* want *a verse to mean to us.*

God designed everything with purpose, from bunnies to beaches to the Bible. It's no good using bunnies for Frisbees or sand for food—and neither should we use the Bible for lucky dipping.

God *intended* what's in the Bible, not whatever we *want* a verse to mean to us. The Bible cannot help us if we cannot understand God's meaning. If we want to have confidence that God has directed us so we can stand solidly on a "word from the Lord," we must begin with what a passage originally meant.

Of course, many find God giving them "a word" without original context. However, their confidence easily shatters when God's "clear direction" grows dim, when they find themselves at a dead end clinging to promises God never made. Learning to read the Bible in context means we care to grow our zeal beyond thin religion. As this chapter unfolds, think of some of your favorite Bible verses and apply them to the principles below. Ask yourself how your favorite snippets of Scripture fit into the biblical story. Such questions show God we want to understand his grand story and how we fit into his world.

Principle 1: Reading in Context

If we want to live biblically and not merely from verse to isolated verse, we must begin with context. Whenever we read a verse, we need to find its "home." For every verse we see printed on a bookmark, a mug, or a plaque, we can ask, "Where does this verse come from?" Finding a verse's home consumes our time, sometimes hours as we read whole chapters or books of the Bible to really understand one verse. But we must invest our time to avoid the temptation of microwaving God's words like spiritual snack food.

If we want to live biblically and not merely from verse to isolated verse, we must begin with context.

In the famous "widow's offering" story in Mark 12:41–44, we both thought that the widow gives us a good example of how to sacrificially give. We've listened to sermons where the pastor taught us that the widow illustrates how giving even when you have nothing left is a sign of faith. We understood that saving for the future was selfish compared to an act of sacrificial giving to God.

Last summer we opened our home for a community Bible study, "Seeing Jesus through the Eyes of Mark."[4] We approached Mark 12 prepared to show how the widow gave sacrificially. But in context, the Bible surprised us and overturned some traditional misconceptions we carried.

We worked out the context with our group by asking, "Why does Jesus point her out to us?" Several replied: "Because Jesus loves her heart." We showed them that Jesus says nothing about his love for her heart. We reminded them to look at the context and note the teaching about the temple before and after the widow's giving.

"A lot of the teachers of the law lacked humility," someone said. "Because the widow had humility she gave everything she had."

"Was it good that she gave?" Dale asked.

"Yes!" a few answered.

"She's like the drummer boy," a woman replied, "playing his drum for Jesus, because that's what he had to give."

A college student spoke up: "I think it's kind of interesting that Jesus talks about the Pharisees always wanting to be noticed, but he notices her and he's the Messiah."

Dale then asked, "In the context, does Jesus commend her for this? Context ... have we heard about widows prior to this verse?" Bible pages turned.

"The teachers of the law devour widows' houses," a woman read from Mark 12:40, a few verses prior.

"Are we witnessing a picture of a widow being devoured?" "Hmms" rippled through the audience, and one college student piped up: "What's the money going to be used for?" Several answered, "the temple treasury."

"The temple, yes," Dale said. "But what's going to happen to the temple?"

A woman's voice rang out. "It's going to be destroyed."[5]

We were all looking at our Bibles now, at Mark 13:2, where Jesus says, "Not one stone here will be left on another, every one will be thrown down."

We realized that all this time we'd admired a widow that Jesus pities. Jesus cares when disenfranchised widows throw money away at ungodly and wasteful enterprises, a place Jesus had called in the previous chapter a "den of thieves."[c] God wants us to invest the resources he's given us wisely, a significantly helpful perspective

[c] Mark 11:17.

if someone were to share that following Jesus doesn't make money sense. Jesus doesn't give foolish money advice. Jesus wants us savvy with our finances.[6] He doesn't want us to give willy-nilly, especially not toward people who devour our money for their own praise.

Suddenly Jesus' meaning became clear to us; we could now see why Jesus highlights this widow giving away all her livelihood to a failing system.

Context expands our understanding of individual verses. To the reader who believes the Bible was written with chapters, verses, and subject headings, hunting for context might feel confusing. But context spills over these man-made boundaries. Chapter and verse markings were not part of the original manuscripts; they were added later, offering address markers to help us quickly find our places together. Chapters and verses should not tell us where context begins and ends. Any time we want to understand context and understand the big picture, imagine no numbers along the margins, no chapter divisions, and no subject headings.

Context works wonders for answering faith questions. Not long ago, when discussing a spiritual book with a friend, we shared why we thought the author incorrect. Our friend took offense that we criticized an idea, saying, "Didn't Jesus say, 'Do not judge!'" He was quoting Matthew 7:1, taking Jesus' words to mean we should not make judgments about others. Jesus did say this, but did he mean we should never evaluate others or offer criticism?

To get the context we have to start way back in Matthew 5, where we find Jesus in the middle of his famous, and often confusing, "Sermon on the Mount." By the end of chapter six, Jesus explains how worry makes us unfruitful. If our Father's love and care extends to hopping birds and waving lilies, it surely covers us too.

Now, we come to Matthew 7:1, and Jesus warns us against judging so that our judgments will not be used against us. Immediately after, in Matthew 7:3–5, Jesus directs this command to hypocritical people, those who have unhealthy, looming issues in their lives, who need to remove planks from their eyes long before they could ever see to help others. Of course, Jesus himself is judging (pointing out) hypocritical people. Could Jesus really be disobeying his own command immediately after he gives it?

In context, "do not judge" doesn't mean we cannot judge good from bad, truth from error, and beauty from ugliness. Rather, Jesus is inviting us to examine ourselves before we judge; we need to know where we stand and unpack our own baggage. When we can see clearly, we can and should help others with proper judgment, pointing out a mistake in order to bear their burdens and help them walk into spiritual health. Jesus could judge the hypocrite because he wasn't blinded by his own hypocrisy.

Jesus is inviting us to examine ourselves before we judge.

The truth stands, even in the twenty-first century. We allow others to evaluate us when we know they speak from a place of health and wisdom. However, if a man in a dysfunctional marriage is leading marriage seminars, we'd cry hypocrite. If a closet liar postured that we should be truth tellers, we'd cry hypocrite. Jesus shows us that judgment from a hypocrite is a contradiction, so he says, "Do not judge."

If we randomly quote Matthew 7:1 without understanding that this verse belongs somewhere, we may arrive at the *opposite* conclusion of what Jesus intends, approving false ideas and winking at human evil, rather than shining a light and inviting others to live well.

Principle 2: The Power of Genre

Jewish agnostic David Plotz read the Bible cover to cover, publishing his amazement and disillusionment in *Good Book: The Bizarre, Hilarious, Disturbing, Marvelous, and Inspiring Things I Learned When I Read Every Single Word of the Bible*. He writes:

After reading about the genocides, the plagues, the murders, the mass enslavements, the ruthless vengeance for minor sins (or none at all), and all that smiting—every bit of it directly performed, authorized, or approved by God—I can only conclude that the God of the Hebrew Bible, if He existed, was awful, cruel, and capricious.[7]

Plotz's Bible reading left him a "hopeless and angry agnostic ... brokenhearted about God."[8] Even reading the Bible in context did not help Plotz trust God's good character. Instead, it left him with evidence that the God of the Bible loved to smite his enemies.

Not every skeptic reads the Bible from cover to cover like Plotz did, but many assume that what they *do* know of the Bible proves it's not worth taking seriously. A friend gave us her rendition of a popular argument: "Christians think you can just take any verse and apply it today. But you really can't take the Bible literally—it says to kill homosexuals[d] and it says to not eat pigs.[e] I mean, come on, have you ever had bacon?"

Unless we can identify and understand the genre we are reading, our expectations can mislead us.

Context is important, but it doesn't always help us understand a verse. My friend and David Plotz would both benefit from a discussion of *genre*. Genre shares the same root as *gender*—*gen*, or "kind." Just as humans come in different genders, so literature is written in different genres. Each genre is defined by certain features and, consequently, must be interpreted with certain rules. Just as we would never search for scientific information about the moons of Saturn in a comic book because we don't expect a comic book to be a scientific guide, neither should we read every passage of Scripture with the same expectations.

Genre creates expectations—and unless we can identify and understand the genre we are reading, our expectations can mislead us. We expect a book on gardening to be a how-to book about plants and soils, not a biography of Shakespeare. If we expect to

---

[d] Leviticus 20:13.   [e] Leviticus 11:7.

get life instruction out of the story of Ruth, we might mistakenly believe that God wants all women to propose to older men. We might "find" things God never meant. When we search some of Jesus' stories for a clear how-to lesson, rather than enjoying their amusing or enlightening social commentary, we are misreading the genre of parable. The Bible, like any other piece of literature, requires us to understand genre if we are to understand meaning.

You may be pleasantly surprised to find you already do this quite naturally. Think of the way we read the newspaper. If the front-page headline reads "Tigers Slaughter Indians," we expect to learn something about large cats attacking people in Asia. However, if that same headline appears on the sports page, we expect to read something about American baseball.[9]

Below we offer several rules for reading genres that have transformed conversations in our own lives.[10]

Narrative

The narrative story of the Jewish people makes up more than 40 percent of the Bible. Basically, if a Bible story can be made into a flannel graph, it's a narrative! Two rules of biblical narrative help us answer those stumpers from people who find the Bible's stories barbaric beyond belief. If you understand the rules of narrative, you can answer questions like, "How can you believe in a book that has polygamy, incest, murder, rape, and racism?"

Narrative tells us what happened, not what should have happened.

1. Narrative tells us what happened, not what *should* have happened. The story of David killing Goliath—while amazing and courageous—does not prescribe how we ought to slay giants, metaphorically or literally. The story of Joseph's coat or Rachel helping Jacob deceive his father tells us what happened, not what God wanted to happen. Bible stories are descriptive, not prescriptive.

2. God is the hero. No matter how magnificently David conquers his giant, David is not the hero; God is. For every biblical

narrative, the hero is the God of Israel, not Noah, Abraham, Joseph, Moses, Ruth, Joshua, or Esther. Even if the biblical story commends someone for their faith, God remains the hero.

Narratives teach us about God even when the people he loves do not obey him (enter polygamy, incest, murder, rape, and racism). Narrative also teaches us why God, not Israel, has the right to condemn those who are guilty. So when God annihilates Sodom and Gomorrah or instructs his people to wipe out another people group, we see a God who claims to be the judge of the earth. What brings God's punishment? Why does he use his chosen people to destroy others? Clues to these questions lie within the larger context.

From a full reading of narrative, we find that God waited hundreds of years before ordering the massacre of people in the Promised Land. He even told Abraham that his descendants would be mistreated as slaves and strangers for 400 years in Egypt, because God could not destroy those living in the Promised Land. Why would God let his chosen people suffer for so long? As God put it, "In the fourth generation your descendants will come back here, for the sin of the Amorites has not yet reached its full measure."^{f} God is not eager for any to perish, willing to wait an extra 400 years, allowing his people to endure slavery to allow the Amorites time to repent. And as we know from Jonah, if any people turn from wickedness, God will spare them. In other passages we find that God did not especially threaten foreign nations and coddle the Israelites. He promised to punish Israel for failing to obey him too.^{g} Read each story completely to gain a front-row seat on how God works, loves, and judges without partiality.

Parables

Similar to modern-day stories that have a moral lesson, such as "The Three Little Pigs," parables are fictional stories that illustrate a point.

---

^{f} Genesis 15:14–16. ^{g} Deuteronomy 28:25–68.

Often parables teach one essential point that can be summed up in a sentence. We don't draw symbolism out of every element. In the story of "The Three Little Pigs," we don't think the pigs' cry, "Not by the hair of my chinny, chin, chin," is an instruction on how to turn bad men away at your door. Every aspect of the story coheres in one essential point: build with sturdy materials. Once we get the main principle, we can apply it in many areas: house construction, marriage, friendship.

Every aspect of the story coheres in one essential point.

Sam Harris, an atheist, lifts a saying of Jesus out of its parable, "But these enemies of mine, who did not want me to reign over them, bring them here and slay them in my presence."[b] In Harris's hands, Jesus looks like a bloodthirsty religious fanatic. Jesus did say this, but Harris doesn't reveal that he found the verse in the middle of a parable. We have to read the parable in Luke 19, using the rule of this genre, to understand the one essential point Jesus is making.

Poetry

Scriptural poetry gives us the words Jewish people prayed and sang. One of the Psalms reads, "He will cover you with his feathers, and under his wings you will find refuge."[i] While this verse is about a literal God who provides real safety, God does not literally have wings. Three common-sense rules of poetry interpretation will guide you to read poetry better.

1. Tools of poetic interpretation teach us to expect imagery, metaphor, simile, and so on. Feathers and wings describe God with a word picture. David's metaphor paints a living picture of how he feels protected and sheltered by God's care. Because we know how metaphors work, we understand that David doesn't think his God is a winged creature.

2. Much biblical poetry is emotional. We must read it again and again, getting into the shoes of the writer, if we want to understand

---

[b] Luke 19:27 NASB.   [i] Psalm 91:4.

the feelings of the poet. Biblical poetry demonstrates that human joy, fear, delight, depression, sexual passion, and even rage are appropriate topics about which to speak to God. Some of Jesus' last words before death echoed Psalm 22, revealing that our Savior relied on poetry to express his own pain.[j]

Biblical poetry demonstrates that human joy, fear, delight, depression, sexual passion, and even rage are appropriate topics about which to speak to God.

Poetry expresses how the poet feels, not how the poet *ought* to feel. If someone accuses the Bible of advocating infanticide, citing the psalm, "Happy are those who seize your infants and dash them against the rocks," we can explain that this poem shares truth about a Jewish captive and his feelings about his enemy.[k] We can even ask them if they've ever felt this way about their enemies, if some people, like Hitler, might have elicited similar feelings. We can also explain God's long devotion to his people—how God will not come crashing in to correct our emotions.

3. Poetry is honest. Look for surprising, shocking bits of real people crafting their feelings into beautiful stanzas. Read Song of Solomon 7:1–9 for an example of unbridled amazement of a bridegroom for his wife's body. Read Psalm 69 for a man hurt and angry at his enemies. Read Psalm 22 for a man in agonizing suffering.

While almost every biblical book includes poetic songs, noted by indentations or stanzas such as Miriam's song in Exodus 15, the Beatitudes in Matthew 5, and the poetic creed in Philippians 2:5–11, you can find concentrated sections of poetry in the Psalms, parts of Job, Song of Solomon, and Lamentations.

How-To

We both learned in high school that the proverbs could neatly fill a whole month by reading a chapter a day. This book offered helpful, quick devotional tips, because Proverbs is wisdom literature, or the how-to genre.

---

[j] Psalm 22:1, Matthew 27:46, and Mark 15:34.   [k] Psalm 137:9.

How-to books, or wise sayings, give us probabilities. So, "A gentle answer turns away wrath, but a harsh word stirs up anger" is true most of the time. If you give a soft answer to an angry person, you will probably turn away her anger. But we've all encountered people whose belligerence remains unstoppable. We cannot take Proverbs as promises, since they never promise a 100-percent foolproof guarantee. They do guide us toward what wise people do and how benefits often follow.

> How-to books, or wise sayings, give us probabilities.

The often quoted "Start children off on the way they should go, and even when they are old they will not turn from it," might tempt Christian parents to feel they've got a guarantee on their children's future. But we all know good parents who have raised their children with instruction to love and follow Jesus, who then watch a child grow up and walk away from God. Often, godly parenting produces adults who love Jesus. But there are exceptions.

Because proverbs are probabilities, we cannot claim them as airtight promises. The wise accept probabilities; a fool ignores them. If we expect proverbs to be probabilities and not promises, we can more easily explain why these wise sayings are not guarantees and explain them to others who question their validity. Wise sayings give us intensely practical, memorable ways to live. But their succinctness comes at the cost of making theological points short and pithy; this genre isn't suited for lengthy theories. Read the Bible's wise sayings in collections to avoid zeroing in on one and making a theological system that contradicts other clearer points in Scripture.

Wise sayings are found throughout Scripture, but they are most concentrated in Proverbs, Ecclesiastes, and Song of Solomon. You'll also find lots of false proverbs in the mouths of Job's friends in the book of Job.

Memoir

In the four gospels, four sets of eyes are trained on Jesus' life with one goal: to introduce various readers to the life, teachings, death, and resurrection of Jesus. The Gospels are memoirs of Jesus' disciples, recording and crafting Jesus' story for a particular audience. Use three principles in reading memoir.

1. Dig around for important background. We all want to be more like Jesus, to have the mind of Jesus, but we cannot take Jesus, who operated in first-century enemy-occupied Israel, and simply cut and paste his life onto our lives in twenty-first-century America. We are not called to walk on water, die for the sins of the world on a cross, or to fulfill a Messianic role. In these ways we cannot be like Jesus the Messiah.

The Gospels are memoirs of Jesus' disciples, recording and crafting Jesus' story for a particular audience.

Memoir both gives background and requires background. To understand the life and times of Jesus, we need to have a decent grasp of the Hebrew Scriptures, Genesis through Malachi.[11] Jesus quotes, relies, and builds upon these texts throughout his ministry, fulfilling what was written in the Law of Moses, the Prophets, and the Psalms.[l]

Jesus offers timeless principles in all his teachings, but we may be mistaken about them if we don't understand his original context. Jesus' teaching may apply differently to our lives than it did to the Jews who heard him. His teaching about paying taxes to Caesar cannot mean exactly the same things to us as we have no Caesar, and we are active voters choosing our governance and taxes. Our reasons for paying taxes may be different, though our priority, that God remains sovereign over Caesars and presidents, is the same.

Get a whole picture of Jesus' teaching by delving into some background reading.[12] This has greatly assisted us in understanding why Jesus said things like, "If your right eye causes you to sin, gouge it and throw it away" and, "The kingdom of God is within you"[m] and why the Pharisees opposed Jesus. In many ways, we've learned that first-century Israel easily compares to our world; we

---

[l] Luke 24:44.   [m] Matt. 5:29; Luke 17:21 NIV

still worry about what tomorrow brings, who we pay taxes to, and if our flesh is too weak. But we differ from Jesus' world, too. For instance, we do not have Roman soldiers demanding we carry their packs for two miles, we can run as representatives of our government, and we have Jesus' power to reconcile us to God.

We must do the hard work of asking, "How is Jesus' situation similar or different from our lives today?" As we learn more about Jesus' time, our investigation will give us ways to apply his words to our day and explain God's ways to our friends.

> *Jesus' teaching may apply differently to our lives than it did to the Jews who heard him.*

2. Each gospel writer wrote to a distinct audience and with a specific purpose. We've found that approaching each gospel with the different thesis statements and backgrounds of each writer in mind helps explain why the gospel stories seem to contradict each other. Matthew, a tax collector, writes to Jews to show them Jesus is the promised Messiah. Mark, probably recording the memoirs of Peter, writes the briefest (and earliest) gospel, revealing in his staccato style Jesus as the suffering-servant Messiah. These two writers use patterns from the Jewish Scriptures to reveal Jesus to Jews. Luke, either a Jew or a Jewish proselyte, writes to reveal Jesus as the Savior of the world and not only the Messiah of the Jews. John tells us he wants to present Jesus as both the Jewish Messiah and the Son of God.[n] As the latest gospel, John uses both Hebrew and Greek thoughts, writing for a wider audience.

The gospel writers use Jesus' stories, teaching, and parables differently, depending on their purpose. They selected and arranged Jesus' words for their audience's needs. The so-called discrepancies between gospel accounts actually indicate God's concern that Jesus' life makes sense to each audience.

3. We must understand the phrase Jesus repeats, "the kingdom of God" (or "kingdom of heaven") if we want to understand the

---

[n] John 20:31.

Gospels. The first words out of the mouth of Jesus in Mark are, "The time has come ... the kingdom of God has come near."*o* For centuries, the Jews had anticipated this moment of God's kingdom breaking into history. With Jesus' arrival the Messiah had finally come to the house of Israel.

Jesus ushers in the beginning of the kingdom of God, a new age that will end with him on David's throne on earth in the New Jerusalem, where all the world thrives under God's government. But first, he dies and rises again to involve his people in his process of spreading the good news—his kingdom is on the move and spreading. As he taught us to pray, "Your kingdom come, your will be done, on earth," we also work to establish God's kingdom on earth.*p*

> *When we watch Jesus walking on water, healing the sick, speaking with authority, we are seeing God's kingdom breaking into the earth.*

What is this kingdom like? Read the Gospels and notice Jesus' work. When we watch Jesus walking on water, healing the sick, speaking with authority, we are seeing God's kingdom breaking into the earth.[13] We cannot lift this phrase "kingdom of God" out of the Jewish context and make it a synonym for an incorporeal heaven. Instead, the kingdom of God is God's government.

The next three genres are not for the faint of heart. These are places we can easily get stuck in conversation. To prepare you to answer questions from any biblical genre, we want to give you some tips for tackling stumping questions from the law, prophets, and epistles.

Law

When a friend lifts a law from Leviticus to prove how outdated the Bible appears, the best way to answer is to share why these laws are in the Bible in the first place.

---

o Mark 1:15.   *p* Matthew 6:10.

Laws reveal God's interaction with broken humans, helping us understand how God wanted a fallen, nomadic people to live in a fallen world thousands of years ago. Laws tell us about God's character, but his laws to the Hebrews are neither comprehensive nor universal. These laws are literal commands to the Jewish people, but God did not intend every human to cut and paste every Hebrew law into their lives. Perhaps we misunderstand that we should, because of our exposure to and appreciation of laws such as the Ten Commandments. But the laws in Scripture are not automatic commands for non-Jews.

To determine what applies to non-Jews today, we need a little background to discover the categories of laws.[14] Biblical law books combine laws for an entire nation about morality, health, civil orderliness, and ceremony all together. Compare what it might be like if a law book in America today listed laws against murder and against jaywalking in one section. One is a moral law, the other a civil law. We know the difference between them in our culture, but people 2,000 years from now may not. If we can cultivate the same awareness when looking at the early Jewish culture, we can share these distinctions when we talk with friends.

While it takes more work to understand the culture of the Jewish people, it is a better and more tolerant approach than dismissing the entire or parts of the Bible as nonliteral.

Knowing the purpose of the law in Scripture allowed us to answer friends who, after reading the laws, thought that the whole Bible was irrelevant. We could point out that there are some laws that do not apply to Gentiles and cite Acts 15:1–29, or that many Jewish laws make perfect sense if you know their background.[15] We can also explain the difference between law as a genre and other genres. While it takes more work to understand the culture of the Jewish people, it is a better and more tolerant approach than dismissing either parts of or the entire Bible as nonliteral. We recommend talking with Messianic Jews for a realistic and respectful understanding of God's Mosaic laws in Leviticus, Numbers, and Deuteronomy.

Prophesy

Prophesy can seem both exciting and cryptic when we try to apply it to our lives. But this genre often gets abused as a guide for what will happen in our near future, quoted with the daily news. It rarely helps our spiritual conversations when we try to motivate others to consider Jesus by painting a modern picture of the rapture. Our credibility as Christians has eroded because of the mishandling of this single genre of Scripture.

More than 90 percent of biblical prophecy outlines Israel's immediate future—events that have already occurred.[16] Prophecy is generally less about *our* future—ancient Hebrews were not writing specifically about twenty-first-century Americans—than it is about seeing how God fulfills his promises to his people in history. Since most of prophecy is about Israel's immediate future, we can keep these four characteristics in mind as we try to better understand God's Word.

> More than 90 percent of biblical prophecy outlines Israel's immediate future—events that have already occurred.

1. God used prophets to warn his people about their unfaithfulness. Prophets were ambassadors from a heavenly court, speaking not on their own initiative, but as God instructed them. They endured hard lives.

Prophets were not welcomed by the people of God as popular or exciting speakers. Israel's kings accused prophets of treachery and banished and imprisoned them. Sometimes prophets shared instruction to submit to their conquerors in order to please God.[q] Little wonder their prophecies required courage and made them unpopular. Prophets didn't invent punishments for Israel; they preached God's message to God's people.[r] As you read proph-

---

[q] Jeremiah 27–28.   [r] See Exodus 3:1, Isaiah 6, Jeremiah 1, Ezekiel 1–3, Hosea 1:2, Jonah 1:1.

esy look for the pattern of Israel's disobedience and God's love. Depending on Israel's love or rebellion toward God, you'll find them experiencing blessing or a judgment.

2. Prophecy will not make sense if you do not understand the covenant that the prophets reference. Authors like David Plotz accuse God of capricious smiting. Yet a little Bible background reading teaches us that Israel willingly entered into a covenant that required specific actions from both Israel and God.[5] Read Leviticus 26, Deuteronomy 4, and Deuteronomy 28–32 to understand the reasons behind Israel's rewards and punishments. Keep the point of prophecy in mind: to remind Israel that they are a covenant people. While it is tempting to interpret and predict unfulfilled prophecy alongside our daily newspaper, we miss the point of God's relationship with Israel. Prophecy is more focused on God's character, justice, and trustworthiness, not about when our world will come to an end.

Yet a little Bible background reading teaches us that Israel willingly entered into a covenant that required specific actions from both Israel and God.

3. Outside reading is enormously helpful. Bible dictionaries or encyclopedias provide the historical setting of each book.[17] Good commentaries like the *NIV Application Commentary* series have helped us navigate each chapter and verse.

4. Prophets often spoke as poets to ensure their messages would ring convincingly and memorably in their oral culture. Therefore, many of the interpretive rules that apply to poetry can help us understand prophecy as well.

Prophecy invites us to notice God at work, to ask ourselves when and why and to whom he spoke. If prophecy distracts us from loving God and others—if we use it as a tool to scare people—then we are misusing this genre. When people misapply prophecy and predict specific events that don't occur, they hurt the credibility of the Bible, not because the Bible was wrong, but because some have

[5] Exodus 24:3–7.

misunderstood the purpose of prophecy as a genre.[18] If "end times" questions and accusations come up, you can share with your friends that even Jesus taught that the date of his return would be unknown.[t]

Letters

Biblical epistles are letters between church leaders and local church bodies. Often Paul, sometimes Peter, John, or Jude, penned these letters. Just like emails today, biblical epistles were written to address a specific person and/or issue. We can often piece together the recipient's locale, customs, struggles, needs, and triumphs if we read each letter in its entirety. Here are some principles for reading these ancient documents more accurately.

Just like emails today, biblical epistles were written to address a specific person and/or issue.

1. If we consider the original audience, we can avoid huge errors of application. For instance, when Paul says in Philippians 1:6, "He who began a good work in you will carry it on to completion," he is not blessing the Philippians with a cover-all expectation that they will grow more like Jesus.

Start by inquiring into what occasioned the letter: Why did Paul write to the Philippians? He wanted to encourage them, as he explains in chapter 1, and he hopes they will realize that their "partnership" in the gospel (v. 5) won't fizzle. We don't learn about what this partnership means until the end of the letter, in 4:14–19. The Philippian partnership is not evangelizing, but financial aid to Paul through Epaphroditus. Unless you read the epistle as a whole, you will not understand that Philippians 1:6 is an encouragement that God will complete the financial-aid work the Philippians began.

Philippi was, as we learn from Paul's missionary work in Acts 16:12, a leading city, a wealthy place for Romans. The Philippian church began in the home of a wealthy woman from a neighboring

---

[t] Matthew 24:36.

city, Lydia. The Philippians most likely enjoyed financially successful members in their assembly and probably cared deeply that their money was being used wisely.

Unless we understand what the original audience understood, we will have difficulty knowing what Paul's words in Philippians 1:6 mean for us. We could erroneously take this verse to mean that our every endeavor is not only sanctioned by God but that God wants us to finish it against all odds.

Sometimes we must read between the lines to discover the needs of each recipient church, but we must always read large chunks of the letter to get at the flow and purpose. As you read biblical letters ask yourself, "What situation is the author responding to?"

2. If we share similar problems as the original audience, then the letter will apply to us in the same way. But if we do not share a similar problem, we will have to do some significant work to mine out the universal biblical principle that we *can* apply to our situation. For instance, in the Philippians 1:6 passage, we are not personally funding Paul; however, the universal principle is that *if* God authors our work, he will be the finisher of our work. A more difficult passage, 1 Timothy 2:15, "But women will be saved through childbearing—if they continue in faith, love and holiness with propriety," plagued scholars for years, mostly because they did not have sufficient background information to piece together the original culture. Scholars tried to untie the contradiction of Scripture as to why a woman would be "saved" by giving birth. But scholarship has uncovered some revealing cultural insight.

Paul wrote first and second Timothy while Timothy was leading a church in Ephesus. Most Ephesian women lived as pagans and prayed to their local, powerful goddess Artemis, the guardian of childbirth in the first century. Paul had a run-in with Artemis' followers when he visited earlier (remember the mob shouting "Great is Artemis of the Ephesians" in Acts 19:28–34!). Writing carefully, knowing the zeal of the Ephesians, Paul's letter underscores how Jesus, not Artemis, offers the *only* power to deliver women through childbirth. We can apply the same principle today for women fearful for their lives and their babies' lives, whether they fear miscarriage or death in childbirth. But without background information we might easily think that women must bear children to earn salvation.

More than any other genre, the Epistles require thorough background reading. While they appear easy to interpret, easier than, say, prophetic literature, theologians Fee and Stuart explain, "The

> *More than any other genre, the Epistles require thorough background reading.*

'ease' of interpreting the Epistles can be quite deceptive."[19] To properly answer key questions (Why did this letter get penned? Who received this letter? What cultural problems or questions were they facing?), read Acts to link Paul's original missionary work with many of the churches he later writes.

Unfortunately, in evangelical culture, we often flip open our Bibles most readily to the Epistles for a quick devotional thought for the day. They appear so clear with commands and pithy encouragement for our lives, "Let everyone be subject to the governing authorities," and "Never tire of doing what is good," and "I can do all things through Him who strengthens me."[u] But as we've shown, the Epistles are not as straightforward as they first appear. Each letter was occasioned by a specific church need and localized in a unique cultural situation. However, if you work to understand the background, you'll find culturally savvy principles that still guide us today. If you're pressed for time, needing a quick devotional, flip instead to Proverbs or the Psalms.

Listing the Genres

We've provided a chart to guide you to each biblical book's predominant genre. Caring about genre will give you confidence

---

[u] Philippians 4:13 NASB.

THE GENRES

Narrative	How-To	Law	Poetry	Memoir and Parable	Prophecy	Letters
Genesis	Job	Leviticus	Job	Matthew	Job	Romans
Exodus	Proverbs	Numbers	Psalms	Mark	Isaiah	Corinthians
Numbers	Ecclesiastes	Deuteronomy	Song of Sol.	Luke	Jeremiah	Galatians
Joshua	Song of Sol.		Lamentations	John	Ezekiel	Ephesians
Judges					Daniel	Philippians
Ruth					Hosea	Colossians
Samuels					Joel	Thessalonians
Kings					Amos	Timothys
Chronicles					Obadiah	Titus
Ezra					Jonah	Philemon
Nehemiah					Micah	Hebrews
Esther					Nahum	James
Job					Habakkuk	Peters
Isaiah					Zephaniah	Johns
Jeremiah					Haggai	Jude
Ezekiel					Zechariah	Revelation
Jonah					Malachi	
Haggai					Revelation	
Acts						

that you're hearing what God really meant to communicate. And your biblical understanding that values context and genre will be a meaningful gift in any conversation.

Putting It All Together

Once you can identify a verse's meaning through context and genre, the individual words within the verse become very important. Most of us easily toss words like "faith" or "sin" or "love" into our conversations, but the Bible's meaning is not always the same as our culture's meaning.

We've noticed that one of the deepest misconceptions about "faith" is that it is "childlike." The phrase "childlike faith" is not in any verse in Scripture, but many Christians believe the concept of childlike faith is communicated in the Bible. As we've asked our friends why they believe faith is childlike and where the Bible teaches this, they inevitably quote Matthew 18:3, "Truly I tell you, unless you change and become like little children, you will never enter the kingdom of heaven." Jesus means, they tell us, that we should have the faith of a child to enter heaven.

Let's apply what we've learned. Since we are in the gospel of Matthew, we are reading Matthew's memoir of Jesus' life. Memoir is the genre. One piece is obvious, "the kingdom of heaven." Remember this is synonymous for "kingdom of God," which Jesus is setting in motion. The Jewish people knew what Jesus meant, not an ethereal heaven, but a kingdom where God reigns, evidenced by the blind seeing, the deaf hearing, the brokenhearted finding hope.

Jesus contrasts the young child to the disciples vying for the best spot in God's kingdom.

Now let's look at the context. In the preceding verses, we see the disciples asking who would be the greatest in this kingdom. Jesus picks up a child playing nearby and puts her in the middle of them all. Then he tells the disciples to change and become like children.

Jesus contrasts the young child to the disciples vying for the best spot in God's kingdom. Jesus surprises them by emphasizing those his society overlooked.

But let's continue with the context. Verse 4 shines an important light on what it means to become like a child. Jesus says, "Therefore, whoever takes a humble place—becoming like this child—is the greatest in the kingdom of heaven."

Jesus highlights the quality of a child we need to have in verse 4. Humility. A humble place. Of course, children are not all naturally humble, but children, especially in Jesus' culture, were easily overlooked and of little account. God wants us to accept who we are within his kingdom, under his reign. He is not asking us to have blind faith or ignorance, which is often what "childlike" means in our conversations. He wants us to become like a young child in our humility.

Through genre and context we clear away some old and popular misconceptions about the nature of the kingdom of God and breathe new life into our conversations about Scripture. Our first step toward the kingdom of God's rule is through humility.

Now let's take a look at what we call the "lost words"—words that have been sullied by overuse and begrimed with misuse.

Chapter 6

Lost Words

I (Dale) sat beside a Mormon man in his twenties on a flight from Los Angeles to Salt Lake City. As we chatted, our conversation turned to religion. He volunteered, "I don't understand why Christians say Mormons are so different."

"Well, there are some major differences," I said.

"But we follow the same Jesus. That should be significant enough."

"Do you mind if I share an important difference?" I asked. When he agreed I said, "Consider the word *dad*. When we say *dad*, we're using the same three-letter word. Yet, that word points to two very different people. For me, it points to a bald guy with glasses from Georgia; for you it points to someone else. It's the same word, but two very different people."

He looked interested, so I continued: "The same is true of the word *Jesus*. When I say *Jesus*, I'm speaking of the second person of the Trinity, God himself, who had no beginning and was virgin born of Mary. Your *Jesus* points to a created being, the brother of Lucifer, the biological son of God and Mary. We may use the same word, but it points to two different people." By the end of the flight, he saw clear differences and had a new look at Jesus.

Words point to things. When we hear *glory*, *sin*, or *faith*, we think about certain ideas, and these ideas change the way we interact with God. Clearly, we need to carefully define terms that are important to our faith, especially when having a conversation with someone who uses the same word but defines the word differently than we do.

Some basic "Christian" words help us know what Jesus is (and is not) offering to us—words which, if misused, make Jesus' good news misunderstood. Five words— *faith, love, sin, forgiveness*, and *glory*— leave many listeners more bewildered than enlightened. Like the word *gay*, which no longer means light-hearted

> *Words don't mean the same thing today as they did in biblical times.*

and happy, these words don't mean the same thing today as they did in biblical times. Their meaning has been buried under layers of Sunday school simplification, modern sloppy use, and political pundits who are biblically illiterate. Yet it is possible to dig down into their original biblical meaning, clean them off, and use them with confidence in our conversations.

Faith: Trusting the Evidence

We've asked teens and adults to explain what *faith* is and have heard a variety of answers, many foreign to the Bible's use of the word. People will say *faith* when they mean the following:

- Sincerely wanting something to be true, such as "I have faith my house will sell."
- A blind leap, such as, "When God doesn't seem to make sense, just have faith."
- Believing with childlike gullibility, such as, "She has the faith of a child."
- Anything religious or spiritual, like when Krista Tippett comes on NPR's airwaves and announces her program *Speaking of Faith.*
- Anything contrary to reason. Mark Twain teased believers, saying, "Faith is believing what you know ain't so."

- Anything that works as a psychological crutch for the weak-minded, helping them get through life's challenges. Atheists and secularists use *faith* this way.

To add to the definitions, a judge in a court of law might refer to an action done "in good faith," which means "acting on good reason." This definition is closest to what the Bible means when it uses the word *faith*. *Faith* means trusting what you have evidence to believe is true. The Bible does not use *faith* to mean childlike gullibility or a blind leap or deep sincerity.

Faith means trusting what you have evidence to believe is true.

For some, considering that faith requires evidence is an oxymoron. But our practical interaction with God proves otherwise. For instance, when God answers your prayers, does your faith grow?"

If we say yes, then we understand that the evidence of answered prayer shows us God is listening and loving. This increases our trust in him. However, if answered prayer decreases our faith, then we would ask God to never answer our prayers. Yet that is backward from what we know of Scripture. Faith in God grows when our prayers are answered. Our faith in God grows, too, in ungranted prayers when we see a better outcome in the future; for even then, we see that God was worth entrusting our prayers to. Faith is growing more trusting of a God who is faithful because he has shown himself to be trustworthy.

Robert L. Wilken, professor of Christian history, puts it this way: "Faith is only as good as its object." If a friend said he'll meet us for lunch at noon, you wouldn't think us ignorant fools for walking toward the pub at eleven thirty. Our faith in our friend makes sense if our friend is reliable. "In good faith" we trust his character. And the more our friend is on time for lunch each day, the greater our faith in his character grows.

Paul makes this interesting point on faith in Corinthians. If God does not exist, if our faith has no real object, our faith is pointless. Paul writes, in 1 Corinthians 15:17: "If Christ has not been raised, your faith is futile; you are still in your sins." God must exist for faith to work as God intended it, or else faith becomes wishful thinking.

Spiritual author Kathleen Norris notes, "No small part of my religious conversion has been coming to know that faith is best thought of as a verb, not a 'thing' that either you have or you don't."[1] Faith is the action of regularly, repeatedly trusting Jesus, who claims to be the truth, and allowing that interaction to spill out in love to others.

Biblical faith takes courage, not because faith is irrational, but because it often requires that we act in ways that may feel unsafe or out of our control. Biblical faith means trusting a God others may not trust. Faith requires vulnerability with God and each other. Guarding ourselves from vulnerable relationships may feel "safer." But guarding also cuts us off from love.

Faith is the action of regularly, repeatedly trusting Jesus, who claims to be the truth, and allowing that interaction to spill out in love to others.

When I asked Jonalyn to marry me, I took an action of faith in her, making myself vulnerable to her rejection. Yet if I remained guarded, never voicing my desire to be with her for the rest of my life, my love would be suspect. That's what James means when he writes that faith without works is dead.[a] Faith calls us to open up our lives to a trusting, vulnerable relationship with a God who has shown us evidence of his life, who delights to direct our steps with his faithful goodness.

When faith is raised in a conversation, feel free to pause and ask, "What do you mean by faith?" That will open the conversation and help you share a clearer view of God.

Love: The Good of Another

After college on the East Coast, I (Dale) moved to Vancouver, BC, to work at a theatre. Each week I carpooled with friends to a

---

[a] James 2:17.

nearby church where I listened to sermons on God's wooing love. God's love opened up new vistas for me. God's love felt like news to me because I had recently come from seven years of living at a conservative Christian college where authorities forced students into submission through a rigid rule-keeping program (reinforced by a demerit system, steady shame and blame for backsliders, and strict chaperoning). That system taught me that God's love came only though his crushing my will, rejecting me till I was fully submissive.

Sunday after Sunday in Vancouver I experienced God's refreshing love, which felt as startling as cool waters. Driving home from church one afternoon, I leaned forward and announced to my friends in the front seat, "Up to now I thought I could only be holy by God beating me into submission. Now I realize God is not like that. His love, his safety, is what changes me. That's what makes me holy."

My friends nodded as if I had shared the most obvious spiritual truth in the world. I chuckled and leaned back again, looking out the window at the city moving past. They had no idea that I had crossed a milestone. I suddenly felt free. I caught a glimpse of a tender God preoccupied not with my sin, but with me, Dale Fincher.

In American culture, we use the word *love* in a variety of ways. We "love" pizza. Grandfathers "love" their newborn grandchild. Junior highers fall in "love." We feel "love" as a surrounding energy of the universe. All of these uses of "love" don't fully capture God's love. We love our pizza because we enjoy the pleasure. A grandfather doting on his grandson, while natural and good, is often happy to return a fussy grandson back to his parents. Junior highers' crushing love is often the awakening of their sexual attraction, a biological, chemical rush. As for the "love" of the universe, spiritual designers have described to us that it gives them feelings of spiritual well-being.

God's love goes beyond these definitions. Scripture explains that love is more than a good feeling; love means we are quick to listen, slow to speak, and slow to anger, setting aside ourselves for the sake of another. Love refuses to leave people alone who've made a mess of their lives. Love does not scold—"You've made your bed,

Love is preoccupied with the spiritual growth of another.

now lie in it!" Nor does love make excuses for people who need to take responsibility for themselves. Love is not content for others to do what they like, rather love is preoccupied with the spiritual growth of another.[2]

Unlike some spiritual designers we've met who say love is an impersonal energy, in the Scriptures, God's love is personal, has a name, and speaks to us. In the Bible, love can only come through persons, whether God or each other.

When we read "God is love," the Bible is not saying that love is God. Nor is it merely saying that God often feels good about us. Rather, God is described by *love*, which means he has the qualities of a loving being, namely, he wants us to grow. He gives us the ability to fill out and grow up into all that we are meant to be. He both knows what's good for us and can accomplish goodness for us.

But God's love is only helpful to us when we are open to him. Because God accepts us so completely, he refuses to allow a corner of our souls to remain hidden and dusty. He will shine a light in to refresh and restore us. His love is not always comfortable, but it is always good.

The Bible drums with the theme of God's love, marching from heaven to earth, God seeking goodness for his people.

- Open your mouth wide and I will fill it![b]
- The LORD, the compassionate and gracious God, slow to anger, abounding in love and faithfulness.[c]
- We know and rely on the love God has for us. God is love.[d]
- "His love endures forever," forms the rhythm of the song in Psalm 136.

[b] Psalm 81:10.   [c] Exodus 34:6.   [d] 1 John 4:16.

Yet we often don't see this kind of love spilling out of our evangelical culture. Perhaps love this lavish feels threatening to good Christian morality. Too often we've heard people say, "Well, yes, God loves them, BUT ..." revealing that love is not our priority. If we take inventory of our ability to love, will we find fear that love will water down the truth? Do we think our acceptance of others will excuse them from growth? Do we think love will teach people to forgo the hard work of repentance? If our answer is yes, we need to rethink love.

Or consider the times we do claim to love but smuggle in other motivations. In the name of love, we ask for other's prayer requests, promising to pray for other's needs, but maybe we're more eager to be first to know the news. We donate our money more because we want the surge of well-being that comes from funding a missionary or youth event. We speak condescendingly toward someone or gossip about their parenting or marriage, disguising it as "speaking the truth in love."[e] We hide behind Bible verses like, "Do not let any unwholesome talk come out of your mouths"[f] to avoid the hard work of loving confrontation, which feels painful and even negative. Fearing rejection, misunderstanding, and causing a scene, we fail to confess our hidden bitterness with the friends we claim to love. We often masquerade as loving people, but behind our masks we avoid plunging headlong into the grit of each other's lives.

We often masquerade as loving people, but behind our masks we avoid plunging headlong into the grit of each other's lives.

But God's love in us will shine to others in a way that marks us as followers of Jesus. Friends of ours had spent years distancing themselves from their gay brother but finally took the loving road of reuniting with him. Their brother accepted them and amazed the entire family with his kindness, sensitivity, and eagerness to be included in the family again. Real love may look differently with

---

[e] Ephesians 4:15. [f] Ephesians 4:29.

different situations, but it always asks us to extend ourselves for another.

It's not entirely our fault that love is difficult to talk about and difficult to live. We've inherited goofy ideas of love from many places: our "Christian" traditions, our modern age that devalues us when we fail, our own tendency to hide and build a fortress around our real selves.

In our premarital counseling, Dr. Jerry Root gave us this simple instruction on love, "Be *scholars* of each other—learn what each other desires and fears." Jonalyn knows my (Dale's) deep need for active listening. I often interrupt her to read a paragraph from a book because I need her to know my thoughts. I've seen Jonalyn drop what she's doing, even when it's very inconvenient, to give me her full attention. In her willingness to give me what she knows I need, to grow and grow together, I feel loved.

Dale knows it's very hard for me (Jonalyn) to sleep while he has his reading light on. For nearly six years he's given up his productive evening reading hours so that we can both fall asleep together. He's chosen to become a scholar of my needs and give me more sleep time, sacrificially releasing his reading time. The result is more hours of sleep, fewer books read, and a very loved wife.

Many needs are hidden, and needs that seem obvious grow more complicated than we first think. Dale has been working on asking if he can interrupt, and I'm ordering and testing out new book lights. We need God's wisdom to guide us into love. All these little acts, creative moments of customizing our love for each other, remind us of the attention God gives us. God loves by not merely giving us warm feelings, but intentionally loving us as a scholar would.

Sin: Twisting Life and Love

"Let's not talk about sin," said one friend of ours. "It's so negative; let's talk about positive things." Many dislike *sin* because it sounds judgmental, negative, hopeless. Careless religious leaders use the doctrine of sin as a bully stick, beating people into repentance or forcing them to try harder. To most people, *sin* only pops up in a conversation to warn them that someone is getting religious.

However, God talks about sin to help us diagnose what's wrong in our lives and in our societies. A friend of ours recently underwent months of testing to diagnose her severe headaches and fatigue. We prayed. Doctors were stumped. She spiraled into depression as she waited in the mystery of what was wrong. Three months later, we received an email: "They did it! They found out why I've been sick!" The wave of relief from this desperate patient reminded us of the value in diagnosis. With a diagnosis, we can launch ourselves on the journey to a cure. Diving into the meaning of *sin* gives us a word to explain the human condition every religion and every spiritual person wants to fix.

God talks about sin to help us diagnose what's wrong in our lives and in our societies.

Despite its popularity in religious circles, sin isn't a *religious* idea as much as a *human* idea. Sin is universal. From our childhood, we begin wondering why we have a hard time making good decisions. Or, as a teenager asked us, "If God wants us to love one another, why is that so hard?" We ignore unpopular people. We tell partial truths and call it diplomacy. We defend ourselves when we're wrong. We seek shelter in meaningless diversions. We fail to love the unlovely. We abuse our power over others. We admit we waste time and need discipline. We don't know how to rest or play without guilt.

In the quiet of our thoughts, we wonder, "How deep does my evil go? If people find out what I'm really like would anyone love me?"

Augustine defined sin as a *twisting of what is good*, like taking the *Mona Lisa* and painting horns on her. Sin takes a good thing, like a chocolate cake, and uses it wrongly, lacing it with arsenic. Sin takes the goodness of sexual passion and uses it for the wrong person, at the wrong time. Sin always preys on the good.

With this perspective, we challenge others who deny the presence of sin in their lives. Don't we all twist and warp the good? G. K. Chesterton found sin such an obvious issue he said it was as "practical as potatoes." If we sin anytime we twist something good, we can begin to realize how God's laws are more than arbitrary rules; they actually safeguard us. We can see how something like the Ten Commandments protects us from twisting our souls and our relationships.

Sin always preys on the good.

Worshiping the true God directs our footsteps; he is a God who goes before us, who guides our future steps and shields us with the love we need. Therefore, God says, *"Don't have other gods before me."* Focusing our attention and resources on gods that lack power and existence perverts our worship and wastes our energy on something that cannot love or aid us.

God gives us time to fill with routine and rest. Because, as James says, our lives are like a vapor, we want to make the most of the days we have.[g] Therefore, God says, *"Remember the Sabbath."* The Sabbath protects us from trampling rest with endless labor, provides time for self-reflection, and relaxes us into the provision of God easily overshadowed by depending too much on our paychecks for our livelihood.

In the Garden of Eden, God gave humans land to steward, animals and trees to tend. Private property empowers us to shelter those in need, to invite friends over for dinner, to steward and pass on a legacy. All ownership comes from God, therefore he says, *"Don't steal."* Stealing twists private property and stewardship that belongs to another and designates it falsely as our own.

Marriage protects two humans in the safety of intimacy so they can plan a life and family together without fear of desertion and competition. Marriage as a metaphor always reminds us of God's exclusive, committed relationship to his people. Therefore, God

---

[g] James 4:14.

says, *"Don't commit adultery."* Adultery pollutes marriage with a third party outside the marriage promise, dishonoring love and the safety of sharing body and soul.

Moral laws help humans live side by side in this world, restraining the sin that blocks us from enjoying the good earth, good relationships, good health. After a Hollywood flick has tricked us into thinking sin is sexy, read a few proverbs to remember how sin causes ruin.[3]

Even apart from religion, many of the laws in our land help prevent us from twisting good things. States enforce speed limits to keep people from twisting cars into weapons. Government enacts clean-air laws to keep corporations from polluting the atmosphere.

Observe the way evil works. Sin appears whenever a good thing is perverted. Sin is unoriginal, leaching out its existence from a good thing God made. Evil can feel good, for a season, because evil things once were good things, before being twisted.

Sin is unoriginal, leaching out its existence from a good thing God made.

Understanding sin helps us explain why our personal evil choices hurt us and others. In sharing with your friends, *sin* doesn't need to be a negative word. It's the diagnosis for what ails humans. With the biblical meaning, we can explain this lost word and more easily talk about a cure.

Forgiveness: Absorbing Evil

One cure for sin is God's command to forgive others. In our everyday conversations we've noticed most people are not familiar with the biblical idea of forgiveness. Some think forgiveness means to forget or to give someone another chance. Others confuse forgiveness with pretending someone's offense doesn't hurt us anymore. We once heard someone say that forgiveness means "for" "giving" someone a big thank-you for teaching us a valuable lesson. But, biblical forgiveness begins with acknowledging someone hurt us, deeply.

Last year, I (Jonalyn) walked through a painful separation with a very close friend. Samantha and I slowly stopped hanging out as I began traveling and speaking more. At the same time she got closer to a mutual friend of ours. A series of misunderstandings grew. I had a long list of offenses, betrayals, and reasons to feel hurt and discarded.

Biblical forgiveness begins with acknowledging someone hurt us, deeply.

When I realized that I only heard secondhand information about her life, her plans to move, her new boyfriend, and her engagement, I realized our friendship was practically over. When I wasn't invited to her wedding but our mutual friend was, I felt she had effectively ended our friendship.

I could have admitted I was angry and wounded. But I wouldn't. I pretended that I didn't care, that I had enough friends without her. I convinced myself that forgiveness means denial, that turning the other cheek meant pretending I was never slapped in the first place.

Deep down, however, I was very upset about losing her friendship. Finally, months later, I brought myself to admit the pain was real and lingering. More months went by in which I fumed, cried, gossiped, and prayed. I had begun the process of forgiveness.

Forgiveness begins when we journey with Jesus back into the memory of the pain. As we name the pain, we often feel worse, even weaker, at first. One sexually abused woman, Linda, tells her story of how revisiting the memory of her sexual abuse brought no desire to forgive. But as she remembered what she had gone through she could see Jesus with her.

In the scene, Linda saw Jesus' anger. "He was outraged over the desecration of her body, just as he was outraged over the desecration of God's temple.[b] She saw Jesus driving out the people who abused her, just as he drove out the money changers who desecrated the temple. Jesus gave her what she needed most: to know how

---

[b] John 2:13-17.

much he loved her in the midst of her hurt and anger, and even to know that her anger was Jesus' anger."[4]

Like Linda, I couldn't just decide to forgive Samantha and be done with it. As Paul told the Colossians, "Bear with each other and forgive one another *if any of you has a grievance against someone. Forgive as the Lord forgave you.*" We must begin by knowing our grievances.[i]

My friend betrayed me.

She made fun of me.

My mother embarrassed me.

He hurt me.

Forgiveness begins as we admit our pain to ourselves, and to God, but not necessarily to the offender. That's how David handled his pain. "They close up their callous hearts, and their mouths speak with arrogance. They have tracked me down, they now surround me with eyes alert, to throw me to the ground."[j] This is not the speech of a man in denial. He spared no details of how he felt and what he wanted God to do on his behalf. Like Linda, he wasn't ready to forgive; but David begins the process by inviting God to see his pain.

Forgiveness begins when we make room for Jesus to sit with us in the pain, feeling our anger with us and guiding us to relinquish our right to exact vengeance.

Jesus showed us that forgiveness doesn't include forgetting or approving the evil. When Jesus hung on the cross, he didn't approve of the embarrassment or the pain he felt. Jesus did not forget who accused him, who tortured him, who nailed him to the cross. Jesus didn't die pretending the evil wasn't so bad. Jesus had the power to face our sin by inviting God into his pain and relying on God's strength to absorb our evil, like blood in a sponge.[5]

Forgiveness begins when we make room for Jesus to sit with us in the pain, feeling our anger with us and guiding us to relinquish our right to exact vengeance. Forgiveness means we refuse

---

[i] Colossians 3:13, emphasis added. [j] Psalm 17:8–15.

to believe the lie that we can remain embittered against someone without harming ourselves. Forgiveness means we invite Jesus' power to absorb evil, releasing the person from our punishment.

Forgiveness requires Jesus' help. We need him so we can bring our sopped-up pain and wring out all our bitterness with him. He wants us to soak up the evil, but not to keep it. In my (Jonalyn's) friendship with Samantha, I began by wringing out all the offenses with Jesus. I told him I didn't feel like I was experiencing his help, but I needed it. I wanted to exchange my heavy load of offense for his lighter one.[k] Absorbing the evil meant I was willing to join in Jesus' work and end the cycle of "an eye for an eye." It also meant I would stop telling everyone else how awful I felt Samantha had treated me.

But forgiveness doesn't automatically restore the previous relationship. People who are dangerous to our physical or spiritual lives cannot be held close in friendship. Jesus didn't trust every person because "he knew all people"; he knew what was in their souls.[l] He purposely taught in parables so only receptive people would comprehend his teaching.[m] He refused to do miracles where people wouldn't believe him.[n] Jesus didn't ask Judas to be with him in those special times, like on the Mount of Transfiguration. Jesus didn't bring all the Pharisees into his cozy group of disciples. Jesus held himself back from certain people, and we may need to do the same.

After I (Jonalyn) admitted to myself that Samantha had hurt me, I felt Jesus asking me to seek reconciliation. I searched in every wedding registry I could find until I found a registry with her name. Then I picked out the most meaningful gift on the list.

I didn't feel excited about giving her a gift for a wedding I was not invited to attend, but I bought the gift anyway. I wanted to act caring even if I didn't feel caring. No matter that one cheek was stinging; I offered her the other. Then, I called her. These steps began a long process of reconciliation. Because Samantha is open

---

[k] Matthew 11:28–30.   [l] John 2:24–25.   [m] Mark 4:33–34.   [n] Matthew 13:58.

to both sharing her side of the story and hearing me out, we are slowly remaking our friendship.

In your conversations, hold to this deeper view of forgiveness that refuses denial, that opens to anger, that invites Jesus in and ends the cycle of revenge. Continue to distinguish between forgiveness and reconciliation so you can present Jesus' way as something both revolutionary and wise. Not only will it help you work through offenses done to you, but it will let your listener see how deep God's forgiveness goes — he asks out of us only what he models.

Glory: Reflecting What God Is Like

We usually think of glory as something only God has, but when it comes to relationships, seeing someone's glory means we see them for who they really are. As Samantha and I (Jonalyn) began to rebuild our friendship we both admitted we saw one another as the enemy, but now we want to love the real person. Our desire is to know the glory of each other.

This word *glory* runs rather recklessly through Christian lingo. We tell young people to consider if they are glorifying God with their music. We pray for God to be glorified in our actions. Often we'll say things like, "God, I glorify you," by which we mean, "I praise you." We speak of God's glory and the glorious future God promises us.

The more I (Dale) read the Bible, the more I struggled with the meaning of *glory*. Glory made me think of blinding bright lights or praise. In Scripture *glory* pops up in a wild assortment of verses that challenge our twenty-first-century understanding. Here's a sampling:

- And I will gain glory through Pharaoh and all his army, through his chariots and his horsemen.[o]
- And the priests could not perform their service because of the cloud, for the glory of the LORD filled the temple of God.[p]

---

[o] Exodus 14:17. [p] 2 Chronicles 5:14.

114

- The heavens declare the glory of God; the skies proclaim the work of his hands.[q]
- The Word became flesh and made his dwelling among us. We have seen his glory, the glory of the one and only Son, who came from the Father, full of grace and truth.[r]
- For they loved human glory more than the glory of God.[s]
- For our light and momentary troubles are achieving for us an eternal glory that far outweighs them all.[t]
- Their destiny is destruction, their god is their stomach, and their glory is in their shame. Their mind is set on earthly things.[u]
- The city does not need the sun or the moon to shine on it, for the glory of God gives it light, and the Lamb is its lamp.[v]

Biblical glory means a weighty presence or reputation, which may not involve bright lights. Try replacing *glory* with *reputation* in all these passages. When we talk about the glory of a person, we're talking about the "weight" of their presence, who they are, what they care about, how they fill a room. The glory of Billy Graham is not the same as the glory of Big Bird. When angels sang about God's glory at the birth of Jesus, they were showing the world the profoundly heavy reputation of God. Giving God glory means we show others God's weighty reputation; it means we show the world what God is like.

> *Biblical glory means a weighty presence or reputation, which may not involve bright lights.*

An Image

Humans were created to be part of God's glory. The Westminster Shorter Catechism says our purpose "is to glorify God and enjoy him forever." Genesis 1:27 states, "So God created human beings in his own image, in the image of God he created them; male and

---

[q] Psalm 19:1. [r] John 1:14. [s] John 12:43. [t] 2 Corinthians 4:17. [u] Philippians 3:19. [v] Revelation 21:23.

female he created them." We are made to reveal what God is like. We're like mirrors made to reflect God through our full humanity.

Sin twisted this task, shattering our mirror. Our ability to glorify God lies in broken pieces. Ralph Waldo Emerson wrote that we are gods in ruins. We still reflect God but in shards.

When Jesus came, he reflected God as humans are meant to—his life was an unbroken mirror, showing us what humans are supposed to look like.

When Jesus came, he reflected God as humans are meant to—his life was an unbroken mirror, showing us what humans are supposed to look like. Not only did Jesus reveal the Father, but he gave us the means and tools to do the same.

I (Dale) remember reading Matthew in a college Bible class, when my eyes slowed on Matthew 5:16: "Let your light shine before others, that they may see your good deeds and glorify your Father in heaven." I'd heard this verse a thousand times, yet slid right over *glorify*. I read the context, saw how the word was used in other verses, and began to understand something meaningful about glory. When we shine the light of goodness, when we live as healthy, loving people, we show others what our heavenly Father looks like. We reflect the weight of his reputation.

Every aspect of our lives gives us a chance to reflect God. In the words of Paul, whether we eat or drink or whatever we do, we do it all for the glory of God.[w] Even the smallest of daily human experiences—eating, drinking, driving our car, getting dressed—are all ways we get to show the world what God is like. Paul shockingly tells us that every act can be an act of worship; every act a radiance of glory. Every day, in every conversation, we can give God glory by letting people see God's attributes in us. If we're glorying God, we're telling others *this* is what God looks like.

In our conversations, we've noticed that explaining the meaning of glory helps our friends see that Jesus wants humans to fulfill their

---

[w] 1 Corinthians 10:31.

unique purpose. So when a mother paints, a farmer tills, a banker invests, for the purpose of showing the world that this is how God would paint, till, or invest, God is glorified. The meaning of glory shows us that God doesn't merely want obedient servants; he wants friends who uniquely reflect the weightiness of God's reputation throughout their own lives.*

Refreshing Words

Uncovering these lost words in our own lives will naturally help us explain the meaning of Jesus' love. Having *faith* means we've chosen to be vulnerable and trust God, who revealed himself to us in the world, through his Word and Son. *Faith*, in turn, opens us to *love*, willing the growth of others and receiving God's friendship. *Sin*, far from being unique and tantalizing, dehumanizes and disconnects us from faith and love, from God and each other. However, we find in Jesus that God is a lover and restorer, healing our wounds, teaching us how to absorb evil and *forgive* as he did for us. *Faith*, *love*, and *forgiveness* each give us ways to shine God's reputation, letting people know Jesus was serious about redeeming our humanity. We can now *glorify* him, reflecting him wherever we go.

These five small, interconnected words paint a picture of what we offer friends. Jesus is more than church on Sunday mornings or a good moral foundation — he offers the only way for us to be fully human.

Now let's combine our tools for reading the Bible and refreshing lost words. This next chapter will help us put our tools in action, giving us the additional tool of paying attention to what some popular spiritual authors are (and are not) saying.

---

* John 15:15.

Chapter 7

Misquoting Jesus

Dale and I (Jonalyn) walked into a deli near the shores of Lake Michigan where a woman with bright eyes and a brusque manner struck up a conversation as she made our sandwiches: "What do you do?"

Dale explained that we run a nonprofit to "help people become appropriately human." We talked about healthy souls, and she shared how she enjoyed studying all the different religions in her college years. I asked her what religion she liked best. She told us none of them. Then I asked what she worships.

She looked up sharply and responded, "I don't worship anything." Here she paused as if gauging her audience's receptivity. "I think of it as, 'I am my religion.'" We made a mental note that "worship" was a churchy word to her and quickly searched for something to give her freedom to continue sharing. We talked about our love for nature until she asked, "So what religion do you like best?"

I answered, "Well, we follow Jesus."

She paused, slapped more mayonnaise onto a sandwich, walked to the back of the pantry, came back, and said, "Well, you've got the essentials."

We've learned to bring up Jesus first and not our denomination, church's name, or even the word *Christian*. Labels have baggage. We don't want to be too quick to slap a label on others because we want to know them individually. For the same reason we don't want to quickly label ourselves and prevent others from knowing us. Explaining that we love Jesus honors people with the clearest, simplest explanation of our allegiance. This is the most straightforward way to learn about someone else's beliefs as well. What do they think of Jesus? The way people use or misuse Jesus tells us a lot about what they think about Scripture, the God of Israel, and the kingdom of God.

> *Even if people don't personally know Jesus, they usually want him on their side.*

Even if people don't personally know Jesus, they usually want him on their side. He offers timeless teachings and an inspiring example. But sometimes people want Jesus' stamp of approval without taking time to understand what Jesus taught.

We've seen people use Jesus' words from Scripture to validate all kinds of ideas; often this abuse of Jesus' words comes from people who should know better—scholars and authors who seek not to understand Jesus but to legitimize their own personal teachings. This manipulation and misquotation often appears in popular spirituality books. We'd like to highlight the work of three popular writers—Rhonda Byrne, Don Miguel Ruiz, and Eckhart Tolle—who are frequently cited as spiritual authorities in our culture. We'll be applying our tools for reading and interpreting the Bible and our new clarity for lost words (like *faith*, *love*, and *forgiveness*) to see how *The Secret*, *The Four Agreements*, and *A New Earth* are less-than-reliable guides for following Jesus.

Unpacking Popular Spiritual Books

Many spiritual people are earnestly, sincerely seeking truth that will set them free. Popular spiritual books can offer helpful insight on how to pay attention to the world, take responsibility, and make plans for your life that fit who you are. When these authors adapt the words of Jesus into their spiritual paradigm, they intend to help people lead better lives. But if they misuse Jesus' life and words, they end up teaching us to misunderstand Jesus, ignore context, and refashion Jesus into our own image.

The Secret

In *The Secret*, Rhonda Byrne writes that the universe can be controlled for our benefit through the "Law of Attraction." If we think about the positive things we want—a job promotion, a soccer goal, a loving mate—then we will attract the desired job, goal, or mate to us. If we use the Law correctly we will get everything we want.[1] The universe becomes a tool to use for our benefit.[2]

Byrne lays out three clear steps from a model of prayer Jesus taught his disciples: Asking, Believing, Receiving. For her, asking means "You get to choose what you want ... like placing an order from a catalogue." Then having asked, you must believe. She says, "In the moment you ask, believe and know you already have it in the unseen, the entire Universe shifts to bring it into the seen." Finally, to receive means we are "feeling good" about what happens.[3] Byrne quotes Jesus as the capstone, showing the reader that Jesus agrees with her, "Therefore I tell you, whatever you ask for in prayer, believe that you have received it, and it will be yours."[a] Byrne teaches that Jesus followed the Law of Attraction.

Let's put Jesus' words in context. In Mark 11 Jesus has just finished a short lesson using a fig tree as an example to condemn the abuses of the corrupt religious leaders. His invitation to pray specifically (ask, believing it will be yours) to God, whom he called Father, means that Jesus assumes a personal God hears our prayers and will work for the good of his people. This is nothing like the Law of Attraction where we expect good things from an impersonal Universe. Nowhere does Jesus suggest we order as if from a catalogue, expecting the mindless universe to shift and bring us whatever we want.

---

[a] Mark 11:24.

In another section, Byrne redefines Jesus' words. Byrne says we should become "childlike," by which she means we should develop a boundless imagination. However, Jesus uses "childlike" to mean accepting your humble place, in contrast to the "greatness" the disciples were asking about.[b] Jesus was not telling his disciples to develop the boundless imagination of children. This is not to say that imagination is an idea Jesus would have opposed,

In speaking with our friends— even Christians!—who live by the Law of Attraction, we constantly ask them to define terms like gratitude and love.

but it's not so much what Byrne is adding to Jesus' words as what she misses. She fails to help her readers see the profound spiritual meaning of becoming as humble as a child.

Byrne redefines key theological words like "faith," "love," and "gratitude" and teaches that "faith" means expecting the universe to respond to your every desire. But Jesus uses "faith" to mean relational trust in a personal God.[c] Byrne redefines "love" as a *feeling* of highest frequency, while Jesus says "love" is doing good to others without reference to feelings.[d] Byrne says "gratitude" means *feeling* glad about our success; Jesus teaches that "gratitude" means thanking the God who supplied the gift.

In speaking with our friends—even Christians!—who live by the Law of Attraction, we constantly ask them to define terms like *gratitude* and *love*. Some have said that the Law of Attraction is similar to the Law of Sowing and Reaping in the New Testament.[e] While both ideas may have similarities, they are not the same. The Law of Sowing and Reaping describes clear cause and effect in the world. If you plant seeds, you get a crop. If you lie to your neighbor, your reputation suffers. The Law of Attraction, however, adds something entirely different. It states that if you imagine something, it will become real to you, like playing make-believe. If you

[b] Matthew 18:1–4.   [c] See chapter 6, "Lost Words," for more on *faith*.   [d] John 21:16–17.
[e] Galatians 6:7.

think of a crop, rows of corn will somehow appear. The Law of Sowing and Reaping, however, requires hard work, not simply our visualization and goal setting, to create new things in the world. The Law of Sowing and Reaping is bound to the causal laws of the world; you put time into plowing rows and reap the final product of a harvest. The Law of Attraction remakes the world to fit any causal laws you can imagine.

To discover if a spiritual author really follows Jesus, check the cited verse's context and refresh the meaning of words with the biblical meaning.

The Four Agreements

In *The Four Agreements*, Don Miguel Ruiz redefines spiritual words by dipping them into Toltec wisdom. Early in the book, Ruiz defines "faith" for the reader. He writes that "to have faith is to believe unconditionally."[4] From the start, Ruiz takes the reader down a path contrary to Scripture, but he claims his ideas are supported by the Bible. However, the Bible never talks about faith as believing something without condition, evidence, or hesitation. Scripture's definition of faith begins with trusting based on evidence.[f]

Upending John's prologue to introduce us to Jesus as the Son of God, Ruiz cites his own version of John 1:1 to prove the power we have with our words: "In the beginning was the Word, and the Word was with God, and the word was God." He adds, "Through the Word you express your creative power."[5] Ruiz explains that John is teaching us to choose our words carefully because our words create our own reality.

However, John isn't talking about words we use in conversation. He is talking about a person—The Word—who is God. John's meaning sparkles with clarity as we read in context verse 14, "The Word became flesh and made his dwelling among us."[g] This Word is Jesus, not merely a word we say to each other. For John, our

---

[f] Again, see page 101 for more on faith.   [g] John 1:14.

words cannot create our reality; instead all of reality was created by God's Word—Jesus the Messiah. Ruiz doesn't read the Bible in context, but he happily lucky dips to show that the Bible backs up his philosophy.

Ruiz also tells his readers they can create their own heaven with their thoughts. He adds:

> Jesus told us about the kingdom of heaven, the kingdom of love, but hardly anyone was ready to hear this. They said, "What are you talking about; I don't feel the peace that you have." You don't have to do this. Just imagine that his message of love is possible and you will find that it is yours.[6]

Notice how Ruiz recasts the *kingdom of heaven* as the *kingdom of love*. Then he tells us the trademark of the "kingdom" is this "feeling of peace." Whenever we read the Gospels, memoirs, we have to remember Jesus' definition of the kingdom of heaven. This phrase means something specific.

When Jesus talked about the kingdom of heaven (Matthew uses the phrase "kingdom of heaven" while Mark and Luke use "kingdom of God"), he meant the literal reign of the God of Israel on this planet, brought about by the Jewish Messiah, Jesus. Jesus opens the gospel of Mark by explaining that the kingdom of heaven is at hand.[h] For many Jesus' kingdom didn't feel peaceful, his kingdom felt like a sword, dividing loyalties and requiring a new kind of citizenship.[i]

By the end of *The Four Agreements*, Ruiz tells us all religions are the same. He says, "This way of life is possible and it's in your hands. Moses called it the Promised Land, Buddha called it nirvana, Jesus called it heaven, and the Toltecs call it a New Dream."

In trying to make a case for his spirituality, Ruiz manages to insult nearly every major religion. Moses, Buddha, Muhammad, and Jesus would all feel misunderstood by Ruiz. Moses believed the Promised Land was a location on the earth along the

---

[h] Mark 1:15. [i] Matthew 10:34.

Mediterranean Sea. Buddha believed nirvana is a state of losing the self into the ultimate reality that unites us all. Jesus taught heaven was an actual place where you awaited the bodily resurrection.

In trying to make a case for his spirituality, Ruiz manages to insult nearly every major religion.

Ruiz, like each of us, can write about his spirituality as he wishes. However, we who call ourselves followers of Jesus need to know if his interpretation of Scripture accurately reflects what Jesus taught. Reading authors like Ruiz will help prepare you to notice the signs when a person is mishandling the word of God. You'll be more apt to notice the same lucky dipping in your everyday conversations.

A New Earth: Awaking to Your Life's Purpose

Eckhart Tolle has influenced millions with his teachings and book *A New Earth: Awakening to Your Life's Purpose*, which Oprah Winfrey featured in her book club. Tolle believes that the universe is an impersonal energy and that our sense of ego, or self, gets in the way.[7] He regularly quotes the Bible, synthesizing Jesus' teachings with his own philosophy.

Tolle tells his readers:

> There is only one absolute Truth ... Yes, you *are* the Truth ... Jesus tried to convey that when he said, "I am the way, the truth, and the life" ... Jesus speaks of the innermost I Am, the essence identity of every man and woman, every life-form, in fact ... Some Christian mystics have called it the Christ within; Buddhists call it your Buddha nature; for Hindus, it is Atman, the indwelling of God.[8]

Read John 14. Is Tolle teaching the same thing Jesus taught?

In context, Jesus is pointing his Jewish students to the God of Israel. Jesus identifies himself as the only way, the only truth, and the only life that can unite humans again with a personal God. Jesus is not promoting a "Christ within" or talking about the innermost "I Am."

Our friend Tony often talks about "Christ-consciousness." Because he sometimes attends a local church, we thought he meant to grow more like Jesus.[9] One day we asked Tony if he could explain what "Christ-consciousness" meant to him. He told us, "Christ-consciousness means abandoning the self and letting your soul disappear into a sea of love."

Jesus is not promoting a "Christ within" or talking about the innermost "I Am."

When we explained to him that his definition would have been a foreign idea to Jesus, that Christ didn't teach anything like that, Tony seemed surprised that we would claim to know Jesus' intention. When we pressed him to study the life of Jesus, he began coming to our Bible study, but even as he learned more about the life and teachings of Jesus, he continued to use "Christ-consciousness" as a prefix for his own views.

We've reminded Tony that he is free to use whatever phrases he likes, but he ought to be aware that this "consciousness" is not what Jesus practiced nor believed as a Jew.[10] "Christ" means "Messiah," which is packed with Jewish ideas about a priestly king who would sit on David's throne. And Jesus never taught us to abandon our individual identities.

To use "Christ-consciousness" to baptize an idea that sounds more like Buddhism than Christianity is as peculiar as using "finding your Zen" to mean passing out tracts for the Jehovah's Witnesses. Zen is not taught by Jehovah's Witnesses; Jesus never taught us to negate the existence of our souls.

In *The New Earth*, Tolle quotes Mark 8:34, explaining that Jesus' call to "deny yourself" actually means "negate (and thus undo) the illusion of self."[11] Tolle invites the reader to practice the mantra, "I Am that I Am" and accept this name of God for ourselves. Tolle's recontextualizing might seem like a helpful commentary unlocking the secret meaning in Jesus' words. However, in context, Jesus' words "deny yourself" do not mean negating the unique person that God has made, body and soul. Instead, Jesus wants us to deny the desire to live life *as we please* and reorient ourselves with God, making his plans our central motivation, even if it costs us our lives.[12]

If we "denied" ourselves in Tolle's sense of the word, there would be no self left for Jesus to save.

In context Jesus asks, "What good will it be for you to gain the whole world, yet forfeit your soul? Or what can you give in exchange for your soul?"[j] He wants to repair our souls, to save our lives, and he uses our desire to keep our soul intact to motivate us. If we "denied" ourselves in Tolle's sense of the word, there would be no self left for Jesus to save.

Furthermore, "I Am" is one of the names of God himself, used first when God spoke to Moses at the burning bush. According to the Bible, no mere human can be the "I Am." Only the God of Israel can claim this limitless, eternally existing title. Jesus used the same title for himself in John 8.[13] Tolle telling us to own the title of God insults both Jews and Christians.

The title for Tolle's book alludes to both Isaiah's vision and John's Revelation, "a new heaven and a new earth." In Tolle's interpretation, "We need to understand that heaven is not a location but refers to the inner realm of consciousness."[14]

In Revelation 21:1, John writes about the new heaven and earth, borrowing this language from another Jewish prophet, Isaiah, to emphasize the physical reality of his point: one day the earth will be restored. Both John and Isaiah believed that earth is our first and last habitation.[15] The Messiah will be in charge, and humans will again dwell on the earth with physical bodies; injustice will be put right, tears will be no more, and the nations of the world will be invited to join in. "Inner consciousness" is not the same as this vision of a new heaven and earth. "An inner realm of consciousness" cannot right systemic, structural, historical evils as God acting as king of this earth will.

These three books we examined above will one day go out of print and new popular books will take their places. Yet when scriptural

---

[j] Matthew 16:26.

phrases appear in new books, we need to remember our tools, pull out our Bibles, and discern whether God's words are being used in context, according to the rules of genre or contrary to the meaning of Scripture. We must be vigilant regardless of whether the author claims to follow Jesus. We will not be working alone. God's Word teaches us that the personal God who inspired Scripture desires that we understand his meaning. As we carefully read the Bible, we will be better equipped to gently recapture the imaginations of our neighbors with the life Jesus offers.

God's Word teaches us that the personal God who inspired Scripture desires that we understand his meaning.

What if we know what Jesus offers but have trouble knowing how to respond when our friends bring up their religion? What can we offer when our friends seem happy with their spirituality? What about the religions that seem so foreign and difficult to understand? We need to expand our tools to understanding how other religions think about the world so we can speak their language more clearly, avoid offensive misconceptions, and share the good news.

Chapter 8

One True Religion?

I (Jonalyn) was having another conversation with my friend, Annie, this time about her boyfriend, a Muslim, who since 9/11 had been banned from flying because he had the same name as a suspected terrorist leader. I couldn't believe he wasn't allowed to board airplanes. The longer we talked, the more the teachings of Islam came into the discussion.

"Muslims aren't violent people—they teach peace. Did you know *Islam* means submission?" Annie asked me.

"That's what they *say* it means. Who are they submitting to? Not the government, not each other. It means submission to Allah."

"So Christians don't believe in submitting to God?" Annie challenged.

"Why do Christians always think that their religion is the only right one?"

I felt stumped for a second. "Christians submit to God, but ..."

Annie interrupted: "Allah is how Muslims say 'God.' It's Arabic for God."

"But they can't be the same God, Annie, because they tell their followers to do totally different things. Like the Qur'an teaches its followers to slay Allah's enemies."

I was about to explain that Jesus says to love your enemies when Annie interjected, "Why do Christians always think that their religion is the only right one? All religions are really teaching the same good things."

Annie is right that Christians think their religion is the right one. But we've discovered that most people believe their religion is right: a Buddhist as well as a Wiccan, Muslim, Scientologist, and Christian. Annie's point comes up often in our conversations. Most people believe that if you boil down each religion to its essentials, each teaches "love, compassion, truth, generosity, forgiveness, tolerance, peace, and courage."[1] If a religion calls God "Allah" or "Vishnu" but still promotes these virtues, it's still spiritually healthy, right? Don't we all want a little more love, forgiveness, and peace in our lives?

Before Diving In

Comparative religious studies make us a bit nervous. Reading apologetic books, preparing rebuttals, or taking an undergraduate comparative religion class is not the same as meeting a Buddhist or Muslim or Hindu.[2] Every person we meet will have a slightly different view on their own religion. Instead of labeling them with what we've studied in books, we listen to them and customize our conversation to them.

In our conversations we've noticed two belief systems, Hinduism and secularism, teaching that all religions are basically the same. We want to compare some significant ways religions are different while highlighting why most people don't know these differences. In our experience, ideas from Hinduism and "thin secularism" work to minimize all religious distinctions.

Instead of pretending all religions offer the same basic ideas, we want to dignify the distinctions between religions, making the most of religious experts when we have an opportunity. At the beginning of a plane flight we were excited that we got the privilege of sitting next to a Hasidic Jew. We thought of some questions to ask him when the flight attendants explained that some people would have to move to the back to balance the weight load. Our neighbor volunteered, and we sadly watched him pack up and walk to the back.

Every fervent religious follower gives us a chance to broaden our understanding. We hope to offer you some tools to give you more confidence to discuss religion with people you might ordinarily avoid.

God(s) Compared

My (Dale's) Christian grandfather contributed to build a chapel at his hometown university shortly before he died. In dedicating the newly christened "meditation room" to my grandparents' memory, the state university chose to write sacred texts from various religions around the walls, each giving a version of the "rule of reciprocity" that Christians know as The Golden Rule. Baha'i prophet Bahá'u'lláh: "Blessed is he who preferreth his brother before himself." Confucius: "Never impose on others what you would not choose for yourself." Muhammad's last sermon: "Hurt no one so that no one may hurt you." An early teaching of Buddhism: "Putting oneself in the place of another, one should not kill nor cause another to kill." Jesus' words: "Do to others as you would have them do to you."[a] While this teaching might help students share sacred space on university grounds, this one moral teaching hardly proves that all religions are fundamentally the same.

Speaker and author Ravi Zacharias, a respected authority on comparative religions, shares another perspective:

> My premise is that the popular aphorism that 'all religions are fundamentally the same and only superficially different' simply is not true. It is more correct to say that all religions are, at best, superficially similar but fundamentally different.[3]

Many American Christians don't know how religions contradict each other. Or we may not believe the differences are all that

---

[a] Luke 6:31.

worrisome, like Elizabeth Gilbert, the journalist *Time* magazine named one of the most influential people in the world in 2008. In her spiritual memoir, *Eat, Pray, Love*, she explains she'll be using the term *God* but that this word is not distinct from *"Jehovah, Allah, Shiva, Brahma, Vishnu,* or *Zeus."*[4] She prefers "God" because it feels natural to her Christian American upbringing, but as she says, "I have nothing against any of these terms ... I feel they are all equal because they are all equally adequate and inadequate descriptions of the indescribable."[5]

> *Many American Christians don't know how religions contradict each other.*

Perhaps because God is infinite we might be tempted to assume he's "indescribable" and unknowable, so we end up thinking God's name doesn't matter. Church praise bands will sing the song "Indescribable," which has given some Christians the impression that God cannot be known at all.[b] Some spiritual designers have told us all the different descriptions of God really refer to the same ultimate reality. However, the evidence we've found points a different way.

Every spiritual person believes God can be described, even the claim "God is indescribable" is to describe God with that one attribute. If you get a Muslim, a Jew, a Buddhist, a Christian, and a Hindu together, each will disagree about who or what God is. The gods are not identical with each other. If all religions' gods were the same God, he would either have a multiple-personality disorder or he is lying. A God like that is unworthy of our worship. We

> *If you get a Muslim, a Jew, a Buddhist, a Christian, and a Hindu together, each will disagree about who or what God is.*

have to do the harder work of respecting the differences of each religion and then determining which, if any, are ultimately telling the whole truth. For each religion teaches different things about who God is, what it means to be human, and how to live a good life.

---

[b] If this is your view, see "God is Love" on page 105.

Is God Personal?

While getting my hair cut, I (Jonalyn) overheard a woman say about her co-worker, "She believes God is personal. I just don't get how people can *still* believe that."

Both Muhammad and Jesus taught that God is a personal spirit with his own thoughts, feelings, emotions, and choices. But when Hindus and Buddhists say *God* they mean something impersonal, very different from what the average Christian or Muslim imagines. *God* will remain fuzzy in our conversations unless we determine what our friends mean and what we mean when we talk about God.

With all the confusion surrounding the title "God," we've been looking for a way to clearly discuss who our God is. In the Bible, God rooted himself into human history by creating a specific people group, the Jews, binding his story on earth to them. God said to Moses, "Say to the Israelites, 'The Lord, the God of your fathers—the God of Abraham, the God of Isaac and the God of Jacob—has sent me to you.' This is my name forever, the name you shall call me from generation to generation."[c]

Whenever we speak of God, we prefer to call him the "God of Israel" or simply "Jesus" to avoid any possible confusion.

Since God has chosen to be the God of the Israelites, whenever we speak of God, we prefer to call him the "God of Israel" or simply "Jesus" to avoid any possible confusion.

The God of Israel personally interacted with his people, giving them specific instructions, inviting them to worship him. In contrast, the ultimate God of Hindus, or *Brahman*, does not personally interact with humans because Brahman is impersonal and does not think, feel, choose, or personally help his creation.[6] At the same time, Hindus believe this impersonal absolute, *Brahman*, lives in every human soul (atman), or as they say, "Atman is Brahman"

---

[c] Exodus 3:15.

(I am Brahman). As Hindu Deepak Chopra writes, "Today I will lovingly nurture the god or goddess in embryo that lies deep within my soul."[7] From our conversations, we've noticed variations of these Hindu ideas coming up while speaking with Wiccans, Buddhists, practitioners of *The Secret* or Kabbalah, and most spiritual designers. Keep an ear out for words like *namaste* or *karma* or "the god within you" to key you into Hindu beliefs in our culture.[8]

Hindus and many spiritual designers take a "both/and" approach to spirituality. When speaking with Hindus we've gotten the impression that they agree with everything Christianity teaches. However, they also (both/and) maintain that God is within all of us, that God is impersonal, and that all other deities—Vishnu, Jehovah, Krishna, Venus, etc.—guide us toward Brahman. One author puts it like this, "Hinduism's supreme being is impersonal, a philosophical absolute, not a personal one. That is why when people ask us who god is, we cannot give a simple answer—god is one, god is all, god is everything."[9] If you're confused or curious about how an impersonal deity dwells within every personal human, we invite you to ask your Hindu or spiritual-designer friends this question.

Hindus cannot tolerate religions that claim to be right.

In our study and conversations we often hear that, "Hindus believe that no religion teaches the only way to salvation above all others, but that all genuine paths are facets of God's Light, deserving tolerance and understanding."[10] In our experience, we have to talk with each person, ask them about who or what Brahman means to them. We've found that when we present Jesus as the *only* way to God, Hindus cannot agree he is the only way. So in some ways, their religion is not "both/and." Hindus cannot tolerate religions that claim to be right. In other words, all religions must become Hindu and nonexclusive at some point to be acceptable to Hindus.

Any time you hear a person claim that all religions lead to the same God, or the same afterlife, you are hearing a doctrine of Hinduism.[11] If Jesus had been able to talk with a Hindu, we imagine he'd respond to their ideas much like he interacted with the Samaritan woman at the well. Jesus models the importance of personal questions when talking about spiritual things.

When the Samaritan woman tries to debate about which worship site is best, Jesus steers the conversation to his uniqueness as living water, offering longer satisfaction than Jacob's well of water.[d] Speaking cryptically, Jesus symbolizes the refreshment this woman craved. Once the woman hears Jesus' unusual offer, she no longer argues about worship sites but says, "Sir, give me this water."

Any time you hear a person claim that all religions lead to the same God, or the same afterlife, you are hearing a doctrine of Hinduism.

Then, Jesus gets very personal, illuminating the issues in her life and her thinking. He alludes to her marital problems and even critiques her theology, "You Samaritans worship what you do not know."[e] He gives her a sure way to align herself with the personal God of Israel and his Messiah. Jesus' presentation offers us a good model: personal, customized conversation that speaks to her real spiritual need.

Talk with Hindus about Jesus' good life, what living water has done for you, before offering arguments about one, personal God. Then ask them to share the benefits of their deity. Do they taste living water in their religion? Do they worship a God who has done things for them? Don't be afraid to point out, as Jesus did, if they sound unsure about what they are worshiping. Be ready to talk about the God of Israel.

The Fatherhood (or Motherhood) of God

We've heard people describe God as the father of everyone. The Fatherhood of God (or, for others, the Motherhood of God) unites all humanity. But not all gods want to be understood as a father

---

[d] John 4. [e] John 4:22.

who relates personally with humans. And even the religions that teach that God is a father don't use "father" to mean the same thing.

Joseph Smith taught that the Mormon God was once a male human. Mormons have shared their popular saying with us, "As man is, God once was. As God is, man may one day become." The Mormon God is a material being who literally sired us. According to *The Book of Mormon*, Father God made physical love to his wife and produced spiritual beings who appear as humans on this planet.

When Jesus called God "Father," he meant a nonmaterial being, eternal, who did not begin as a human. He said, "God is spirit," not matter.[f] Because he has no body, God has no more maleness than femaleness. Jesus taught that God created all things, not that God sired each of us. Jesus' disciples wrote that we become children of God, not physically, but relationally. God "gave [us] the right to become children of God—not children born of natural descent."[g] "Born again" doesn't mean that God births us, but that God adopts us.

When Christians say Jesus is God's only begotten Son (quoting John 3:16), they do not mean God sired Jesus. When Jesus calls God his Father, he isn't saying that God the Father had sex with his wife to create him. As Jesus put it, "I and the Father are one in essence."[h] "Father" signifies, as the Christian creeds teach, Jesus' relational dependency on the Father in his earthly life, not biological dependency.

Distinct from Mormons and Christians, Muslims would never call Allah "Father" because to a Muslim, "father" means a strict biological relationship. Allah is not Father because Muslims are not considered his children.[i] In speaking against Christian doctrine, the Qur'an teaches Jesus is not God's son, It is not worthy of the Beneficent God that He should take (to Himself) a son."[12] "He begets not, nor is he begotten."[j] Muhammad taught that Allah's

---

[f] John 4:24. [g] John 1:12–13. [h] John 10:30. [i] Surah 5:18. [j] Surah 112:3.

uniqueness is totally incomparable to us. To associate God with anyone else, such as believing God is three in one, is blasphemy.[k]

Distinct from Mormons and Christians, Muslims would never call Allah "Father" because to a Muslim, "father" means a strict biological relationship.

In contrast to the transcendence of Allah, some Wiccans teach that a female Goddess exists close enough to be part of us. Depending on the Wiccan you talk with, her tradition might call the divine "Mother" and "Father" while believing that both dwell within us as divine energy. The Goddess, sometimes called "Mother Earth," exists as part of the earth's creativity, goodness, and life. And as earth dwellers, Wiccans believe we are all a part of this divine essence.

In talking with friends of these faiths, keep the idea of "father" in mind. We ask people to explain what they mean when they talk about their God and offer these examples of what religions mean (or refuse to mean) by "father" to show differences. Asking for clarity and underlining some differences allows us to begin to understand and respect distinct religious teachings instead of assuming we are all really worshipping the same deity.

Doing Good for Different Reasons

My (Jonalyn's) grandparents' native language is Spanish. As they learned English, they better understood the uniqueness of Spanish because they knew another language. In the same way, we understand the uniqueness of our religion better when we develop a deep and sympathetic understanding of another person's religion.

We're able to recommend Jesus' command to "love your enemies and pray for those who persecute you," because we know how distinguished his teaching looks next to, say, the Hindu teaching of unattached good works.[l]

A Hindu and a Christian might approach a thirsty beggar on the side of the road with the same offer of water. But the committed Hindu

[k] Surah 4:48, 171–72, and 5:72. [l] Matthew 5:43–48.

will be acting out of one of their Holy Books', the Bhagavad-Gita, command to practice "disinterested action," renouncing any rewards that come from their kindness.[13] The Hindu doesn't offer water in order to join Brahman's plan for the earth.

The committed Christian acts out of the many commands to help the needy. For instance, Jesus' command "Whatever you did for one of the least of these brothers and sisters of mine, you did for me."[m] The Christian offers water because he wants God's glory, to make God's reputation great and join Jesus in his plan for this earth. Christians look forward to the proper rewards for their action, things God promises, like the fruit of his Spirit.

Since many religions end up doing good in the world, it's easy to assume we are all motivated by the same reasons. We realized how inaccurate that is when a Buddhist in our town showed up on our porch one evening. We had commissioned him to do some work on our fence several months ago, but after agreeing to begin we didn't hear from him again. He said he wanted to apologize for leaving us hanging. When we thanked him for following up, he added, "I just didn't want the bad karma from leaving a job unfinished." We realized that while he was doing the right thing, his primary motivation was to protect himself, not to be kind. Granted, Christians often do the same, like seeking forgiveness to clean up their reputation. However, Jesus asks us to do good to our enemies and forgive those who hurt us not merely to clear our name or eliminate bad karma. Jesus said, "But I tell you, love your enemies and pray for those who persecute you, that you may be children of your Father in heaven."[n] Jesus asks us to forgive because that is what God does, and when we forgive we are acting as children of our God.

In our recent dialog with several Buddhists from Thailand we realized that they practiced meditation to avoid suffering, to gain happiness, and to increase their overall desire for purpose in their lives. In our lives, we practice meditation on Scripture and silence in prayer because we want to know God; we want to listen to his

---

[m] Matthew 25:34–46.   [n] Matthew 5:44–45.

ideas about our lives. Happiness and satisfaction are often natural by-products of our time with God, but we do not meditate on God's Word primarily for happiness.

You will find it helpful to ask your friends to explain why they practice their version of spirituality. Inquire into their motivation to help the needy, to attend their mosque, to sacrifice at that shrine, to visit their ancestors' graves, to volunteer at the hospital. What is their religion offering them? At the same time ask yourself the same questions.

To assume that all religions are the same insults every religious person, patronizing their reason for conversion.

These differences between religions do not automatically mean other religions are wrong. But to assume that all religions are the same insults every religious person, patronizing their reason for conversion. We do not want to treat our friends as if their spirituality could be interchanged with any other.

Thin Secularism

We said earlier that Hinduism and secularism are two beliefs that lead people to think all religions are basically the same. We spoke about Hinduism above. Now we turn to secularism, often the main reason people in American culture say all religions are basically the same.

Many people are not concerned whether their religion is true, so pointing out differences in religions may be uninteresting to them. As one friend explained to us, "I was looking for the religion that felt like home to me and the practices of Islam just fit. I belong there; it helps me connect to God."

Many think of religion like a sport. Just like you can choose between many sports for physical exercise, people feel they can choose between many religions for spiritual exercise. If you tend to treat religion as a private affair, something to do on your days off, something too private for the marketplace or political discussion, you may actually be dabbling with secularism.

Secularists are not the new kids on the block. No matter how "Christian" we think our country once was, we've always lived in a secular land. Austin Cline, a director for the Council for Secular Humanism, says that "secularism argues generally for a sphere of knowledge, values, and action that is independent of religious authority."[14] In principle, secularism seeks common ground through tools of reason, history, science, and common sense without imposing religious laws or holy books. Separation of church and state has evolved into a secular idea to protect everyone's freedom of conscience, implying that no religious institution can be controlled by the state and vice versa. While perhaps appearing to be the enemy of Christianity, secularism has the potential to preserve human dignity and expand our freedom without bloodshed. For example, secularism permits churches the freedom to practice the Lord's Supper or to raise children in a variety of ways without sanctioning or controlling one way as more godly.

Many think of religion like a sport. Just like you can choose between many sports for physical exercise, people feel they can choose between many religions for spiritual exercise.

Many Christians we've spoken with blame secularism for many of society's ills, citing things like removing prayer from public schools as the beginning of America's slide from God. We were both raised among churches where people feared God would remove his "blessing" on America due to our country's immorality and irreverence for the God of the Bible.

Nevertheless, upon studying secularism, we do not believe all secular people can be blamed for America's moral failures or for suppressing the efforts of religious and spiritual people. In a pluralistic society, where many religious people mingle and seek to live together peaceably, our public policy has to be built on ideas accessible to all people.

We see some benefits in secularism. Secularism has strict rules that stretch us to redevelop our arguments. Secularism insists that we avoid carelessness when we apply the Bible. Secularism requires that if we speak about God's existence or the morality of helping the poor or the problem of abortion or gay marriage, we cannot argue *exclusively* from the Bible or from the basis of any other religious book or institution. If we believe abortion damages mother, father, and child, we may let the Bible inform us, but secularists will insist we do the harder work of finding reasons and evidence that appeal even to a nonreligious person.

Secularism says we cannot argue exclusively from the Bible or from the basis of any other religious book or institution.

However, here's the more interesting point: the secularism that muzzles many Americans today is not pure secularism. A thinner, less robust version currently overshadows the original open-minded premise of secularism. Just like "thin religion," which does not rely on a full understanding of sacred writings, so "thin secularism" is a belief system that doesn't understand the rules of pure secularism.[o]

Thin secularists do not allow religious discussion in public, even when the religious idea is based on reason or common sense or any other publicly accessible idea. Thin secularists believe that if an idea is religious, it must remain private, personal, subjective.

Thin secularists believe that if an idea is religious, it must remain private, personal, subjective.

We saw thin secularism at work when Michael Newdow appealed to the Supreme Court to remove the words "under God" from the Pledge of Allegiance. John Ziegler interviewed him on KFI in Los Angeles. The poised and articulate Newdow insisted that since our First Amendment says Congress shall make no law respecting the establishment of religion, "under God" should be removed from

---

[o] See page 77 for more on "thin religion."

the Pledge of Allegiance. Why? As he put it, because "God is a religious idea."

Newdow's logic is correct. If God is merely a religious idea and if the First Amendment says the government cannot promote religious ideas, then "under God" should be removed. However, Newdow was wrong to assume that God is a religious idea.

A thin secularist overlooks how easy it is to believe in God without adhering to any one religion. Philosophers, including Plato and Aristotle, argued that God existed without reference to any religion or holy book. Any secular philosophy professor knows the arguments for this "god of the philosophers." Today even most nonreligious people believe in God because philosophy, history, experience, and even certain assumptions in our scientific method open the door to his or her existence.[15] If we have evidence that God exists apart from religious authority, then God is not "merely" a religious idea.

If we have evidence that God exists apart from religious authority, then God is not "merely" a religious idea.

Pure secularists understand this. As a secularist, Thomas Jefferson, who coined the phrase "separation of church and state," could still refer to the "Creator" in the Declaration of Independence. He justifies a Creator not with a verse from a holy book but from his human reason. Pure secularism permits our currency to be stamped with "In God We Trust" and our politicians to sing on the steps of the Capitol "God Bless America" after the 9/11 attack, both appropriate secular expressions as they do not point to any religious institution nor exclusively endorse a single religious book. Including "under God" in our Pledge of Allegiance follows in the tradition that pure secularists have always allowed.

Religion: Sport or Medicine?

We mentioned earlier that a thin secularist will choose their spirituality not because it is true, but because it is helpful. They think of religion as sport: as long as we receive spiritual exercise, why push for your spiritual "sport" over another?

One way we can begin to talk about religion with a secularist is to suggest that religion may not be like a sport, where you can choose whichever works for you. To use another metaphor, religion has historically been thought of more like a remedy, or a medicine for what ails humanity, than a sport to keep us spiritually toned. Just as we want the best medicine to soothe our sore throat, we want the true spiritual antidote to our spiritual ailment.

To introduce religion as a type of spiritual medicine, ask your friends what they believe is wrong with this world. Ask them to explain the disease and hatred, the corruption and poverty. Once you can discuss the problems in the human condition you can more easily compare the different solutions among religions. You can then recommend Jesus' solution to the ailment, or sin, he found in all people. You can suggest that Jesus wanted to set people free.[p] You can let them wrestle with his words, "No one comes to the Father except through me."[q]

Religion has historically been thought of more like a remedy, or a medicine for what ails humanity, than a sport to keep us spiritually toned.

You might want to refer to historical figures who relied on their religion not because it kept them balanced or peaceful, but because it offered them truth and direction in the world. At the Reformation, Martin Luther did not question the Church's authorities because he thought this would bring him more peace. Quite the reverse, he knew questioning would bring discord and pain into his life. But Luther wanted truth; he wanted to follow his God-given faculties of conscience and reason; he wanted the true antidote for what ailed the Catholic Church. And when bullied to recant, he famously said, "Unless I am convinced by Scripture and plain reason ... my conscience is captive to the Word of God. I cannot and

---

[p] John 8:32.   [q] John 14:6.

I will not recant anything, for to go against conscience is neither right nor safe. God help me. Amen."

To the early settlers of our nation freedom of religion meant that they could worship the way they found true without being discriminated against and killed. Throughout history, religion has always been of interest to the seekers of truth. Each person's religion is the best medicine they have found for the spiritual ills of their life and this world. You wouldn't say to someone with an ailment that as long as they are taking medicine, any medicine will do. Neosporin will not stop a headache. We do not want to capitulate to thin-secularist ideas and prescribe to the deep ailments of human evil a wide variety of spiritual solutions, especially when they contradict each other.

Why is it that religious ideas are no longer treated as true or false in our public conversations? To begin with, thin secularists often wed themselves exclusively to science. If something cannot be tested under a microscope, then thin secularists doubt whether the claim can be known. To many people, knowledge from the humanities, philosophy, and theology doesn't count as real knowledge. So unless science can prove a religious claim, spirituality becomes a matter of opinion, something we follow either because our parents taught us, our culture believed it, or we just found it helpful. The last thing a thin secularist wants to say is that spirituality can be true.

Can a religion be right or wrong?

When we realize a friend is a thin secularist, a good question to ask is "*Can* a religion be right or wrong?" If they answer no, then you can ask them if even fundamentalist terrorists can be right. Most will say a fundamentalist can't be right, which gives you an opportunity to reexamine the question again. Apparently some religions can be right and some can be wrong. Ask them how they judge between what is a right religion and what is wrong. They may end the conversation with, "What is true for you may not be true for me." And we can follow Manner #7 and let them remain unconvinced. But as we model true godly tolerance, they may start to think about the issue more deeply for the first time.

Because history is rife with examples of religious persecution in the name of God, we understand the uneasiness some thin secularists might have when religious institutions exercise power in public policy or when a religion claims it is the right one. But as we learned in manners of loving discourse (Manner #4), just because people abuse God, doesn't mean we judge God by this abuse. Evil acts are performed by atheists and secularists as well. The deeper, more valuable, questions remain, "Can a religion be right or wrong?" and if so, "How do I discover it?" When our friends come to this question, we can link arms with them as we push into knowing God.

Tolerance

One tangible example of thin-secularist ideas changing our culture is how quickly people stop talking about religion when they're accused of being intolerant. We've watched Christians silence themselves after such accusations. Since many other religions tend to think of Christians as intolerant, we need to analyze if the charge is accurate and if so how we can respond. What is tolerance? Is it something Jesus asks out of us?

Tolerance in its original sense involves two necessary experiences. First, we experience something we don't like, such as a grain of sand in our shoe rubbing a raw spot. Second, we extend patient endurance toward the unpleasant thing. So if we're walking up the beach to our hotel, we may endure or tolerate the grain in our shoe until we walk into the lobby, where we can remove the sand. Tolerance means we choose to live with something that disagrees with us.

Tolerance means we choose to live with something that disagrees with us.

Tolerance is only a virtue when we endure something disagreeable, painful or false. We tolerate a foul-mouthed teenager when we listen to their language and try to understand them. We can love them and still disapprove, but tolerance teaches us to share our disapproval while still treating them as a valuable person. We tolerate a child's bad manners, especially when the child is not ours. We tolerate a buzzing fly while we write a letter, not because the fly doesn't bother us, but because we have to exercise long suffering to endure its distraction.

You cannot practice the virtue of tolerance unless you are bothered. We cannot tolerate another religion if we agree with that religion. But if some aspect of a religion bothers or concerns us, we can truly tolerate it. Tolerance means we listen to someone else's beliefs even while we may believe they are inaccurate, even while we hope that they will be nudged closer to another view.

Tolerance means we will still listen to their rejoinder and love them in return; it does not mean we celebrate all their spiritual views. Many thin secularists confuse tolerance with approval; they assume tolerance means we never critique another religious point of view. Thin secularists often condemn any critique as if we were attacking a person, which is both hypocritical as they attack to keep us from critiquing, and inconsistent. We know it's possible to love a person as fully human and still critique an inconsistent belief, like when I (Dale) critiqued Jonalyn for buying uncomfortable shoes, after several years of tolerating her complaints after long walks. In the same way we tolerate our Buddhist friends when they tell us that common sense cannot be relied upon. Tolerance means we keep listening and waiting to see if they want to hear another perspective.

A healthy person speaks up against bad behavior and false ideas when the time is right. Jesus did. If you take time to notice Jesus' godly tolerance, you will see his timing is always impeccable. For example, before the Sanhedrin and Pilate, Jesus tolerates a string of lies and remains quiet, but at another time, before the Sadducees' questions, he corrects them, "Are you not in error because you do not know the Scriptures or the power of God? . . . You are badly mistaken!"[r]

---

[r] Mark 12:24 and 27.

On a recent blog post, a reader left a comment that I (Dale) was judgmental for writing that Buddha's teaching was dehumanizing. Instead of showing how I was wrong, the commenter simply said to "judge not lest ye be judged," which was a judgment using my Scriptures against me. The commenter was also playing by the rules of thin secularism, telling me that any judgment between religions was immoral. He wasn't comfortable with my critique, but instead of showing why my idea was wrong, he attacked me and told me not to judge.

Notice how people will cry "intolerance" and tell you to not judge when they want to avoid God talk. In the hands of thin secularists, tolerance has become warped. Tolerance may well become an excuse to not interfere in the lives of others, to wash our hands of the choices others make by remaining silent when it comes to spiritual conversations. But, if we don't believe religious differences matter, it's not much of a virtue to tolerate the differences. Kenneth Woodward, *Newsweek*'s thirty-eight-year religion editor, writing for the *New York Times*, explains how thin secularism or, as he calls it, *today's* "religious tolerance … comes easiest to the religiously indifferent and to the condescending."[16]

> *We believe all humans benefit when religious followers bring their spirituality into their public world for discussion and critique.*

We believe all humans benefit when religious followers bring their spirituality into their public world for discussion and critique. Christians are well-suited to revive the practice of proper, respectful tolerance, given our example of Jesus, who graciously loved and tolerated many false beliefs and ugly behaviors. As we strike up conversations with the cashier at the grocery store, or our server at a local restaurant, we need to be mindful that tolerance listens well and shares without censoring others. A good test to verify if you're being truly tolerant is to observe if your conversation partner feels free to disagree.

Our best conversations come from our honest sharing about how we've found our religion and spirituality true, not just true for us, but true for everyone. Only when we've taken our religion that seriously can we discuss the real religious differences. We must do additional work, wrestling on our own, stepping into the shoes of those who believe differently, to see whether their beliefs make sense, set us free, and help us love God and each other.

Talking Like Jesus

With many thin secularists telling us to keep our religion private, it's easy to feel like bringing up God is as unwelcome as talking about an embarrassing relative. Because many of us are rusty when it comes to talking about God in the marketplace, in public areas, we want to recommend you retrain yourself to use the same dignity of language God used for himself in Scripture.

In Scripture, God claims to be the God of a nation, not a God of a privatized, personalized spirituality. He says, "I am the Lord; that is my name! I will not yield my glory to another or my praise to idols."[s] Jesus spoke like he offered a real solution (the kingdom of God) to public and private problems.

When Jesus calls us to follow him, he isn't offering a daily spiritual regimen to help us find a little bit of peace and balance when things get tough. Jesus does not present himself as one of many viable options to the Jews or to the Gentiles. In the Gospels he claims to be the source of light for the entire world.[t] Jesus speaks with urgency, as if he was the only source of life, truth, and goodness. He's speaking into the real human need, declaring himself as vital as daily bread and living water. He believes we are people made to be fully human, created to endure forever. Jesus never intolerantly forces others to believe him or trust him, but we cannot deny that Jesus assumes his life is for everyone.

Now let's see how we can begin to talk about the God of Israel like Jesus did.

---

[s] Isaiah 42:8. [t] John 12:46–49.

Chapter 9

The Hope for Human Healing

As I waited for Dale to collect me at the airport, a man with tired eyes approached. He told me of his mind-blowing experience in India and how he was free to love and offer peace to anyone at this airport. I listened and asked a few clarifying questions until he began asking me to buy some of his books. The one he held out boasted a blue-skinned god (Vishnu) with four arms surrounded by several women on the cover. I told him I wasn't interested in buying or taking the literature. When he pressed me, insisting that I accept his offering to avoid bad karma, I explained my main problem with karma.

"I have a hard time believing karma is really the way the world works. Someone molested my close family member when she was five years old. Karma says she deserved this from a previous life. Does your religion say that a child deserves to be molested?"

My argument hit a sore spot and the tone of our conversation deteriorated. He raised his voice, gesturing largely, and ordered me to accept the book because he had a quota of books to hand out. I took a copy, looking down at the book for a moment, breathing a short prayer for wisdom. When I looked up he was already walking away, talking with a couple. I wondered how much my question would help his journey. Did he know how other religions explained suffering? I wish I could have shared another option.

Every religion offers an explanation and a specific remedy for the world's suffering. Every religious founder tried to point to the root of humanity's problem. Buddha called it desire.[1] Hindus call it ignorance or a poor memory.[2] Jesus and Muhammad called it sin.[a]

Even today, religion mixed with thin secularism offers pervasive do-good maxims to guide us out of the evil around us.

The atheist's version: Do good for goodness' sake.

The legalistic Christian's version: The joy of the Lord means a smile on your face.

The secular version: Do something good every day.

The Hindu's version: Become virtuous by virtuous action.[3]

Pop spirituality's version: Be positive and practice random acts of kindness.

Even our decorations offer do-good maxims: Live well, laugh often, love much.

All good thoughts, but how on God's green earth do we do all that? Would we be equally inspired with a reminder that says, "Get yourself a million dollars"? It's a nice idea, but how? Announcing something we all want is not the same as having it or helping us get it.

Fixing What Ails Us

All religions agree that humans are incomplete and that we need something more to be healthy and loving. Wiccans, Hindus, Muslims, Buddhists, and even atheists claim that humanity can, somehow, overcome its deficiencies. Here are a few distinctions on how different religions claim to restore our humanity.

Wiccans, in general, believe humans can achieve serenity and

Announcing something we all want is not the same as having it or helping us get it.

All religions agree that humans are incomplete and that we need something more to be healthy and loving.

---

[a] See page 107 for more on sin.

harmony through communion with the divine energy of nature (many Wiccans teach that everything is part of the divine) and practicing virtues, including love. Assisted by reincarnation, this is the hope for restoration of humanity and the earth.[4]

Many Muslims believe humans are born naturally submissive to Allah but prone to rebellion. Through submission to Allah and faithful practice of the Five Pillars of Islam, humans overcome evil within them and the world. The only restoration of humanity is acceptance of good works by the mercy of Allah, so that we can one day be free of the earth and enter Paradise.[5]

Because atheism is less codified, atheists' views differ. However, many atheists believe humans are not born morally broken but become evil through horrible circumstances and inhumane socioeconomic conditions. Most atheists believe more scientific education and economic reform will permit our inner goodness to shine through. We can restore our original, good humanity if we throw off the escapism of religious "superstition" and deal with life head-on.

Hindus believe that we all long to escape the cycle of reincarnation, to rid ourselves of our karmic debt through following *dharma* (the correct understanding of reality, differing according to each practice), paying karmic debts, and appeasing and following certain Hindu gods. Through these steps each person can restore their soul and escape from human bodily experience.[6]

Buddhism explains that previous lives have created all kinds of evil, sickness, and personal and social harm in our present lives. While Hindus believe the individual person works out their karmic debt through reincarnation,[7] many Buddhists teach that the individual person is only an illusion, only the karmic debt is transferred in each rebirth.[8] Buddhism teaches that the Eightfold Path gives us the tools to work out both good and bad karma to reach our ultimate human end, which is to lose our human distinctions (including gender, personality, community) in nirvana.[9]

The Christian must also ask where evil originated. If we blame the sinfulness on our parents, then we ask where they inherited it. And if we keep tracing the question far enough, we find ourselves at the story Jesus taught. According to the God of Israel, the human problem began in the Garden of Eden when our first parents disobeyed and chose the knowledge of good and evil over the love of God. They chose self-rule over God's rule. They believed they could handle the fruit of the tree because, through the serpent's arguments, they thought God's divinity was their own. But by taking of the fruit, they were scorched by the knowledge of good and evil. Since then, evil has been ubiquitous in both ourselves and our world.

Jesus taught that we live with evil and self-centeredness in our hearts. "For out of the heart come evil thoughts, murder, adultery, sexual immorality, theft, false testimony, slander."[b] According to Jesus, the human problem that lives inside us is beyond our powers to fix. Our humanity could only be restored when an uncorrupted, fully human person comes as an example and sacrifice, not only to break the evil within but to empower humans to become fully human in relationship with God and others. Jesus *empowers* us to do what many religions only *tell* us to do: grow in love, discipline, and truth. In Christianity, as in all religions, good works are important, but these good works don't earn the love of God, they evidence the love of God working in us. And unique from all Eastern religions, the end of humanity is not an escape from the earth but a remaking of it.

> *Jesus empowers us to do what many religions only tell us to do: grow in love, discipline, and truth.*

Healing Human Weakness

I (Jonalyn) have a Taoist friend, Chris, who owns a jewelry shop in Los Angeles. I've spent hours working on beaded projects while

---

[b] Matthew 15:19. See also Mark 7:20–22 and Luke 6:45.

discussing spirituality and philosophy. One afternoon I asked him a question that the ancient philosophers asked: "What do you do about your human weakness?" The question works well in moving the dialogue from intellectual possibilities to actual personal experience. We recommend it for anyone who is a deep thinker about spiritual things. Here's how the conversation unfolded.

"What do you do about your human weakness?"

"You know how we all have problem areas that trip us up?" He nodded. "So what do you do when you find yourself returning to the same mistake again and again? What do you do with the failures?"

He thought for a while and shared how he sometimes has a short fuse. He counts to ten, breathes deeply, and tries to remember that anger never accomplishes anything.

"But don't you find yourself continuing to fail again?"

He confessed he did. At this point, I realized that Chris sounded a lot like many Christians. We all have our issues and we're all trying hard to change, to be better people. Most of us don't ask God to help us every time we mess up. Taoism was not different, especially since Taoists don't believe in a personal God. Taoism offered Chris coping instruction for handling his temper, but it left him cycling through anger and calming exercises over and over again.

"Don't we expect our religion to help us to find a way to change, not just cope?"

I wanted to point this out, so I asked, "Wouldn't it be wonderful if you didn't get all hot and bothered in the first place? Don't we expect our religion to help us to find a way to change, not just cope?"

He stopped working and looked up at me. "Yes, that would be nice." He shared how desire really is the root of all evil, and if he didn't care so much he wouldn't get angry.

I listened, nodding while he talked. Then, I gently explained how I could not agree with him, pointing to all the beautiful precious stones around us. They were desirable, lovely, and good. Wasn't it good to desire beauty?

"Yes, beauty is good." He was silent as we both continued stringing beads together. Then he turned to ask me, "What do you do with the areas that trip you up?"

His question left me feeling unprepared. I knew that there were the standard moral answers like memorizing Scripture and making new resolutions, but every religion offered that. Didn't Jesus offer us more than tips for controlling our vices? How could I communicate this?

Taking Our Medicine

We (like most Christians) believe Jesus died for our sins, that Jesus made friendship with God possible. We know Jesus offers real solutions to our problems.

But for most of my (Jonalyn's) life Jesus has been like a bottle of medicine I carry. I have faith that his medicine works; I've memorized portions of the Bible (like the medicine's instructions) so I can share with others. I've even talked about how Jesus makes my life better. But unless I open the bottle and take the medicine, ingesting it into my blood, Jesus cannot fully heal me.[10] Today, Christians call this process spiritual formation.

In order to answer people like Chris, we need to take the medicine. We have to revive an old Christian discipline of including Jesus in the everyday moments of our lives. The Catholic monk, Brother Lawrence, learned to invite Jesus into every moment, from washing dishes to saying prayers.[11]

We've been trying to invite Jesus to accompany us in working on our computers, in answering the phone, working in the garden, meeting a friend for coffee. When we feel lustful, we invite Jesus into our sin. When we feel sick, we invite Jesus into our suffering. When we worry, we invite Jesus into our anxiety. Inviting Jesus into every moment is not magical; the prayer merely opens us up, so we are willing to notice how he wants to help us. Inviting Jesus into our daily moments means we invite him over to sit with us, suffer or smile with us.

Through this practice, we've seen Jesus change lifelong patterns of sin in both of us. Like a few months ago when I (Jonalyn) went out to lunch with a girlfriend. While eating I suddenly realized I was only half listening to my friend. The other half of me was subtly trying to catch another man's attention, to get him to notice me—a man who wasn't my husband. Instead of berating myself for being flirtatious or lustful, I simply prayed, "Jesus, I invite you into my lust." I went back to my conversation, expecting Jesus to help me where I was weak.

In a flash, my eyes were opened. It wasn't that the man across the restaurant became ugly, I didn't suddenly stop wanting to notice him, but Jesus altered the way I saw him. I noticed, for the first time, the woman who was sitting across from him, the elderly man sitting beside him. I imagined him a son, a husband, a father. I saw him as a man made in God's image, not a man I wanted to tempt or attract. Jesus saved me from my vice, again.

We need help to will the good, to feel the good, to love the good, and to become good.

Jesus promised that his salvation, like medicine, must work from within us. "Remain in me, as I also remain in you. No branch can bear fruit by itself; it must remain in the vine. Neither can you bear fruit unless you remain in me."[c]

So next time, when Chris shares how overwhelmed he feels, or how easily angered he becomes, I will tell him about Jesus, who doesn't simply leave us with good principles like "Close your mouth and count to ten before speaking." Jesus will make his home inside us, loving us, so that he can renovate our souls. If we want to ask him to heal us from something, he will sit with us in the puddle of lust or envy or pride. He will help us out.[12]

---

[c] John 15:4.

Without Jesus, we cannot fully fix all that is broken in us—false beliefs, evil thoughts, deceitful emotions, poor choices, chaotic desires. Society, parentage, education, abuse, and misery in this world often train us to hide our soul's sickness. Many Christians—we know because we used to live like this—try to bear fruit without Jesus. We need help to will the good, to feel the good, to love the good, and to become good. We need to abide in Jesus, every day, praying for him to supernaturally change us. The change is slow for most of us because our habits and false beliefs run deep.

Jesus' closest three friends experienced this need for God's power. On the eve of his death, Jesus asks his disciples to pray for him. He returns to find them sleeping. He says to Peter, "Simon, you went to sleep on me? Can't you stick it out with me a single hour? Stay alert; be in prayer, so you don't enter the danger zone without even knowing it. Don't be naïve. Part of you is eager, ready for anything in God; but another part is as lazy as an old dog sleeping by the fire" (MSG).[13]

Only one religious founder claims that no matter how good you become, you cannot mend your essential brokenness by yourself.

Even Jesus' disciples had to pray for God's help, and they lived with Jesus for years. They knew all of Jesus' teaching, but they had to ingest God's power through prayer. Without Jesus we cannot be ready for what God wants us to do.

Only one religious founder claims that no matter how good you become, you cannot mend your essential brokenness by yourself. Help cannot come from inside of us. Jesus says, "I am the vine; you are the branches. If you remain in me and I in you, you will bear much fruit; apart from me you can do nothing."[d] Meditate on John 15 and how Jesus' love changes us. On our own we cannot repair our broken desires. Jesus taught that we need the personal God of Israel to meet us and empower us to know what humans

---

[d] John 15:5.

were meant to be. As Bono of U2 puts it, "You see, at the center of all religions is the idea of Karma. You know, what you put out comes back to you ... And yet, along comes this idea called Grace to upend all that 'as you reap, so you will sow' stuff ... Love interrupts, if you like, the consequences of your actions."[14]

In pouring out grace, Jesus reflects the way the God of Israel has always acted. Though we do reap what we sow, taking the consequences for poor decisions, Bono, the modern psalmist, would direct us to Psalm 126:5: "Those who sow with tears will reap with songs of joy." Jesus accompanies us and turns our mourning into dancing. Jesus is the author of grace in our lives.

The way of the God of Israel, shown to us in Jesus, stands distinguished from other religions. Most Eastern religions, other than Islam, teach us to "awaken" or to "follow these simple rules" to "visualize the goal," to "meditate on your divinity." They teach us to try harder with a little more "letting go" or "killing the ego." But Jesus does not offer mere practices and maxims, he offers himself. He reaches into our souls and mends us where our methods and efforts cannot.

But Jesus does not offer mere practices and maxims, he offers himself.

Watching Jesus Work

Micah was a high school student whose eyes flickered with both eagerness and a hard coldness. In his late teens he wanted to commit suicide, but he found counselors and friends who helped him seek Jesus and claim the value of his life.

He explained to us how he had intentionally tried to follow Satan in high school and did nearly everything parents pray and hope their children will avoid. After a shocking experience with the God of Israel, Micah began to follow Jesus. As he put it, "I thought of myself as a Christian and a fairly righteous person. So yeah, I have some problems and pet sins but doesn't everybody?

And anyway I'm better than half the people out there. I don't have any major sins."

But Micah needed more than a one-time prayer of allegiance — he needed to be apprenticed by Jesus. Micah told us:

I really, truly, don't "get" this Christian "thing." I want to follow Christ, but I totally don't understand how. I feel like Paul most of the time. I do things I don't want to do, I regret doing them, am genuinely sorry, and then I go and do them again. And I am trying desperately to figure out how to live. How to find the abundant life in Christ. But I don't really know what that life looks like. The church tells us to look like Jesus, but how do you do that?

Unfortunately most of us are puzzled about this question too. We have trouble bringing up Jesus in our conversation because we're not precisely sure what he offers us besides heaven and a community that holds us accountable to good morals. We're simply not sure what other good news Jesus was talking about. How is he any different from another prophet or religious teacher? How do I (Dale), a twenty-first-century Gentile, look like Jesus, a first-century Jew?

Here's how one of my online conversations with Micah grappled with that very question.

Dale: God didn't make us to be Jesus; he made us to be ourselves. Jesus is the answer to help us be ourselves. The results will be different for each person ... Peter is different than Paul is different than Matthew is different than John ... etc.

Micah: Ohhh! See I have been wandering around trying to figure out how to be Jesus. Isn't that what the church teaches? But I can't be Jesus, because I am not God. So, the goal of Christianity is to allow Jesus to help us be ourselves? Not to demand Jesus conform us into being Jesus?

Dale: I think that's the biblical view. Being "like" Jesus just means learning to see the world the way he does, having sound character, a strong will that knows the good and does it ... etc.[15] Being "like" Jesus means being dependent on the Father. But it doesn't mean "becoming" Jesus ... there is only one Messiah!

Micah: The idea that "Jesus is the answer to help us be ourselves" makes a great deal more sense. And seems significantly more possible than trying to be Jesus ... Figuring out how to be Micah, I can do.[16]

Trusting Jesus to be his deliverer was just the title page of Micah's spiritual life—now he's learning to be the Micah God has built him to be.

Being "like" Jesus just means learning to see the world the way he does, having sound character, a strong will that knows the good and does it ... etc.

Conversations about Jesus aren't meant to climax with a decision to "ask Jesus into our hearts." If we need a goal in our conversations—beyond seeking truth together and loving each other—the goal is this: we are making students of Jesus. Not in a formal "let's meet every week and I'll mentor you into better behavior, being a better Christian, fitting in with our church culture" sense, but in a relational "tell me about Jesus in your life" sense. Discipleship means inviting others to share the life we enjoy and regularly experience under the tutelage of Jesus.

People often wonder if we're committed to one religion or denomination. "We both follow Jesus," we say. "We think he was on to something." That's the best hope for human healing we've yet to find.

Let's now turn to some popular topics and hot issues that arise in our conversations, many of which keep people from seeing Jesus clearly.

Part III

Helping Friends Home

Chapter 10

Mountains That Are Molehills

I (Dale) grew up in a family that resisted alcohol. My church discouraged any alcohol consumption, explaining it as a "worldly" practice that tainted our "testimony."

Plus, I saw consequences of a family member hitting bottom after years of alcohol abuse. As he entered a tough-love rehabilitation program for alcohol and substance abuse, I watched him and the many others in the program struggle with quitting an addiction. I saw the heartache in my family. I saw the difficulty of starting up life again and fully healing. So I decided to steer clear of the unnecessary fruit of the vine.

However, years later, during premarital counseling, our highly respected Christian counselor recommended that Jonalyn and I enjoy a glass of champagne on our honeymoon. His idea, combined with Jonalyn's freedom to enjoy wine on occasion, helped me rethink a more nuanced position, not judging alcohol by its abuse (Manner #4).

Though inside the church I was taught that alcohol would give Jesus a bad reputation and would wreck families, I later learned that outside the church, proper use of alcoholic beverages does not taint a reputation. Most believe wine and beer offer great human pleasures to be enjoyed. Sometimes the religious restriction of alcohol hurts Christians' reputations more than responsible drinking.

As I rethought my position, I discovered that Scripture did not forbid wine in most circumstances; even the psalmist says God created it to make the heart glad.[a] I've since changed my stance on the issue, seeing wine as a gift from God. And like all gifts from God, sometimes abused.

Historically, Christians have turned consumption of alcohol into a major taboo, turning an area of freedom into a social barrier between Christians and people outside the church. We meet people pleasantly surprised and relieved to find serious Christians unopposed to drinking.

To drink or not to drink alcohol, while a worthy subject for careful thought, is not an essential doctrine of our Christian faith.

To drink or not to drink alcohol, while a worthy subject for careful thought, is not an essential doctrine of our Christian faith.[1] Alcohol is a molehill that many Christians have made into a mountain. Instead of welcoming someone into fellowship with Jesus—and trusting God to begin informing that person's decisions—sometimes we force that person to climb the mountain of our personal morality, expecting and inspecting the fruit of conversion prior to conversion. Sadly, some give up on the journey before ever seeing Jesus.

Molehills—arguing the credibility of Jonah and the big fish, sweating out small errors in Scripture, insisting upon six-day creation and the permanence of hell—make for fascinating, heated debate points, but ultimately are nonessential doctrines. They are not beaches to die on. We are *not* saying these issues are irrelevant, nor that Christians shouldn't hold firm views on them. But debate about these topics is often best left to intramural discussions between Christians.[2] If we argue about evolution or the dangers of a Corona with those who do not know Jesus, our conversations end up missing Jesus altogether. It's amazingly easy to be sidetracked. Sometimes we forget we're inviting people to Jesus and not to our brand of Christianity.

---

[a] Psalm 104:14–15.

As trained apologists, we love exploring nonessential questions so we can deepen our trust in God. Yet, we've been tempted to require our friends to agree with our views of nonessential doctrines. When we prevent others from seeing the diverse views available to Christian brothers and sisters, we're replacing the true rabbi. Discipleship means that we follow Jesus and trust his schooling when differences arise.

In the next chapter we'll discuss some molehills our culture views as mountains: hypocrisy and sexism in the Bible, homosexuality, and abusive spiritual leaders. We need to know how to talk about such hot-button issues with love, grace, and truth. For now though, let's turn to some important side issues we've overblown into pillars of the Christian faith. By moving beyond these nonessential issues to focus on the larger issue of Jesus, you'll enjoy more fruitful spiritual conversations.

In every personal conversation with those who have never considered Jesus, we want them to see Jesus, not mountains and molehills.

Was Jonah Swallowed by a Whale?

Once upon a time a Jewish prophet ran away from the God of Israel because he refused to share God's love with Israel's enemies. God, however, employed an unlikely chauffeur—a massive fish—to steer Jonah in the right direction.[b]

The Jesus conversation was in danger of being eclipsed by a smaller story.

While I (Dale) spoke to a group of college students about Jesus, a student suddenly blurted out, "Well, what about Jonah and the whale? That couldn't have really happened!"

Red herring alert! A "red herring" is a distraction that leads us away from the main point. The Jesus conversation was in danger of being eclipsed by a smaller story. Because Jonah is part of the

---

[b] Jonah 1.

Bible and Jesus is part of the Bible, it would be easy to think that we must defend *any* Bible question before we can talk about the topic at hand.

Do not feel the pressure to follow the red herring.

We do believe Jonah was swallowed by a huge fish, mainly because Jesus believed it too. He even used Jonah as a metaphor for his own resurrection[c] and compared himself to Jonah as a symbol of God's compassion and justice.[d] But the life of Jesus and his work are not dependent on the story of Jonah and the whale. Let's introduce people to Jesus and his resurrection before getting sidetracked by Jonah.

Prepare yourself to hear mention of biblical stories in spiritual conversation and to dismiss them as distractions from the main point: the day the sun stood still for Joshua, Moses parting the Red Sea, the command against eating shellfish, the rape of Dinah, and whether Cain married his sister. None of these questions need to be answered definitively before we introduce our friends to Jesus — and if someone insists that they do, ask them why. Sometimes this is a real hurdle; often this person is more interested in arguing details than in meeting Jesus.

When questions like this distract us, we'll often say, "For now, let's set aside the question of whether or not that happened. Let's talk about Jesus and see where that leads us." If that is acceptable to them, you can continue with the main point.

What about Errors in the Bible?

When someone points out a seeming discrepancy in the Bible, we understandably make a mountain out of this molehill because we think God's Word is in danger. If we hear a form of the accusation, "Since the Bible is written by humans, it has to have errors," we feel like our entire religion is suspect. We start defending the Bible

---

[c] Matthew 12:40.   [d] Luke 11:29–31.

for all we're worth. Popular books like Dan Brown's *The Da Vinci Code* stirred up a lot of conversations when he suggested that the church corrupted the real gospels and suppressed the true teachings of Jesus.[3]

There are many ways to respond to such suggestions. One of the most effective ones we've used is to begin by granting the possibility of errors. This disarms our listener, causing them to realize immediately we don't hold on to our views blindly. Suppose real errors do exist. Suppose something troubling has been uncovered in the pages of Scripture. Does this mean the Bible is *completely* false or that Jesus isn't worth following? Should we discount Einstein's paradigm-shattering theories of relativity because we discover a few errors in his notes or calculations? Announcing that possibility allows the conversation to relax a bit, taking each "error" on its own merit.

We believe the Bible is without errors in the first editions, in the original documents penned by the original authors.

Let us be clear: We believe the Bible is without errors in the first editions, in the original documents penned by the original authors. Our modern Bibles are derived from overwhelmingly consistent copies and fragments of these original documents. We will, however, admit that not every insight into historical background, cultural meaning, and archaeological location has been discovered. Years ago archaeologists disputed the existence of civilizations named in the Bible, yet now we have archaeological evidence for their existence.

From this position of overall confidence, we can admit that the Bible holds some tricky passages that puzzle even the most astute scholar. Consider, for example, something simple: the number of horsemen David took from Hadadezer. One verse says he took 700.[e] Another says he took 7,000.[f] Some look at discrepancies like these and say, "The Bible *can't* be true if it contains errors!"[4]

---

[e] 2 Samuel 8:3–4.   [f] 1 Chronicles 18:3–4.

Take a more complicated example: Jesus said the mustard seed is the smallest seed on earth.[g] Yet smaller seeds exist, like the poppy. If Jesus were speaking as a scientist in our day, he would be wrong. But he was simply using it as a metaphor based on knowledge common to his audience. He couldn't introduce a smaller seed for his metaphor if his audience didn't know about this seed. The point of his metaphor was to describe something else. These common examples are bandied about on skeptics' blogs and in atheist chat rooms as reasons to doubt the Bible's trustworthiness.

Be encouraged: You do not have to answer every attack on the Bible.

Be encouraged: You do not have to answer every attack on the Bible. It isn't your job to *prove* the Bible is free of errors. Let the molehill remain a molehill. Your job is to love others and introduce them to Jesus, not to lecture them on the intricacies of historical canons.

In our conversations, we never try to prove the Bible's inerrancy, not because we believe the Bible is erroneous, but because other topics, like the resurrection of Jesus, are more important. The number of David's horsemen is a molehill compared with the towering mountain of God's love coming to earth.

For some skeptics, however, the presence of *any* error in the Bible means that *nothing* in the Bible can be trusted. (This position is usually held without a great deal of self-reflection, considering we *all* put trust in historical facts and sources that are significantly less well attested than the Bible.) If someone refuses to take anything in the Bible at face value, we argue for how *reliable* the Bible is in important matters. We say, "Don't think of the Bible as a holy book just yet — let's evaluate it as a historical book, a record of what many people saw. Let's require the Bible to meet the same standard we use for other historical works and biographies." This allows our friends to look at the Bible again, with less suspicion. We then explain how the Gospels are ancient memoirs.[h]

---

[g] Mark 4:31. [h] See page 87 on the memoir genre.

If our friends appear interested, we can talk about the reliability of multiple witnesses. If one morning paper said five thousand people attended a political rally and another says ten thousand attended, would we say the rally never happened? In the same way, if one gospel says one angel was at the empty tomb[i] and another gospel says two angels were at the empty tomb,[j] should that distract us from noticing the empty tomb?

When speaking about Scripture to those who suspect its validity, we need to focus on the Bible as a reliable guide giving us the person and teachings of Jesus. Remember to ignore the red herring to *prove* all of Scripture inerrant.[k]

What about Evolution?

Many Christians consider it impossible to believe in the God of Israel and the authority of the Bible while also believing in evolution. According to their thinking, evolution is incompatible with the words of Scripture, and evolution makes religious morality and faith in God untenable. From the way certain Christians talk, Creationism is Christianity and evolution is atheism.

However, evolution is not synonymous with atheism. Atheists may claim that it is, and some Christians may argue that it is, but evolution, a historic/scientific description, cannot dictate what we do with God.

> *From the way certain Christians talk, Creationism is Christianity and evolution is atheism.*

Evolution explains *how* our universe came to look like it does through natural processes, not *why* the universe exists. Similarly, *how* we arrived at the party isn't as crucial as *why* we came to the party. Evolution, as a scientific theory, need not concern us as much as philosophical naturalism, a 2,300-year-old belief that only the natural world exists.[5] While a philosophical naturalist cannot

---

[i] Mark 16:1–8. [j] Luke 24:1–8. [k] See page 209 for more on reliability.

believe in Jesus' message, an evolutionist can—and tens of thousands already do.

Several years ago, I (Jonalyn) gave an address at a secular university. My topic, "How Christianity Gave Women a Soul," attracted lots of women. One undergraduate introduced herself afterward as a biology major and launched into a serious dialogue.

"I get what you're saying. Jesus is for women and cares about women. I like that. But how can you believe he's God? That seems totally bizarre. I'm an evolutionist and it's weird to think of God on earth."

"I don't think evolution is a barrier," I explained to her. "You can follow Jesus and still believe in evolution—lots of Christians do. I think the issue is philosophical materialism."

"Okay, I haven't heard of that. What is it?"

"Well, naturalism, or philosophical materialism, is the belief that matter is all that matters. Everything that exists can be boiled down to molecules and atoms. Everything outside of matter doesn't exist, including God, angels, souls, and love—unless you're talking about the hormone oxytocin!" I smiled and paused.

She was following me intently. Without cracking a smile she said, "Okay, I don't think I believe in philosophical naturalism because I'm pretty sure something is out there."

"Well, if this Something exists," I said, "Wouldn't you expect it to be pretty big, powerful, maybe even good?"

She nodded, "Yeah, *if* God exists, he would have to be powerful."

"In your study of biology, does it make sense to think that if God exists, he's probably behind the stuff you're learning about?"

"You mean like he created everything?"

"I'm not saying God made every cell by hand, or even each species." I reiterated, "God could have used evolution. Regardless, evolution needs a starting point. Call it the big bang, or whatever, but *something* started *everything*. This something is what I call God."

"Okay, so God started the process of evolution?"

"It's possible. And that gives us some ideas about what God is like."

"What do you mean?" she asked.

"If God can create a process like evolution, he's smart, and he might even communicate with the world."

"Why?"

"Don't you like interacting with the stuff you've made?" I asked her, "Isn't that what parents say about their kids?"

"Okay, I know you said in your talk that God made humans in his image, so that means some things about us are like God. Do you think God used evolution to make people too?"

"I think God could use evolution to produce humans who have some resemblance to God." I clarified, "I don't mean we *are* God, just that we reflect some things about God. Like I said in my talk, we're little pictures of God. We reflect God, like a mirror. God is love, so humans love too."

"Right. God is love—that fits," she smiled.

"That's our connection! If God is love, we'd expect God to love and interact with the earth and maybe even give us some tips about how to make sense of this place. God might even visit."

"That's the Jesus part?" she asked.

"Exactly."

As Christians sharing God's love with the world, let's refuse to give evolution the power of disqualifying someone from following Jesus.

If I had argued against evolution, this conversation would never have included Jesus without feeling like a tacked-on sales pitch. This young woman already had an embryonic belief in God, but her interest could have died if she'd been forced to choose between God and the science that fascinated her.

Regardless of our views of the scientific theory of evolution, all Jesus followers believe God created and sustains this world.[6] Whether or not evolution accurately describes the history of life on earth doesn't alter the evidence that Jesus rose from the dead or that God is the originator of all things, seen and unseen.

As Christians sharing God's love with the world, let's refuse to give evolution the power of disqualifying someone from following Jesus. Let's focus our conversations on the *why* of life here on earth and be ready to tell the story of the reasonable hope we have in God.

Why Did God Create an Eternal Torture Chamber?

Christianity is often ridiculed in America as the only religion with a wrathful God who sends people to be tormented in hell. Because modern evangelicals were born from revival tent meetings in the nineteenth century where hellfire was a clear motivation for conversion, our gospel message of "going to heaven when you die" can feel like a push to make a decision for fear of the afterlife. A bumper sticker we recently read stood up to this, stating, "I believe in life *before* death."

We are leading people to Jesus, not to our brand of Christianity.

We recently spoke with a woman who for years devoted herself to Christian work. Yet she gave up on Christianity because she could not accept the idea of endless hell. Her story is far from unique. Who can stomach a God who tells us to love *our* enemies yet casts *his* into an endless fire? How can God be called just if he punishes our measly eighty years of earthly sin with a permanent torture chamber?

How should we address these questions? Our solution is relatively uncontroversial and needs repeating: We are leading people to Jesus, not to our brand of Christianity.

Followers of Jesus who take the Bible seriously hold different—sometimes widely different—views on hell. Some say hell is a garbage dump (a metaphor Jesus used)[7]; some say people may not stay there forever, or that all will eventually leave; others teach that the damned may cease to exist.[8] Some think that hell may be locked from within,[9] or the gates of hell are wide open but nobody is willing to overcome the dangerous and painful process of leaving.[10] Some say hell is another word for alienation, a place where people become trapped in the desolate dungeon of their ego.[11] Some say hell is the only place we can be "safe" from God's pursuing love.

When a seasoned executive we met on a plane told us adamantly that hell did not exist, and that *everyone* goes to heaven, except for Hitler, we noticed the red herring. We chose to steer the conversation back to asking him who God was in his life. What ways had he experienced or longed for God's love? What makes people, we asked him, refuse to let God work in their lives? What creates a Hitler? We would do well to follow Jesus, who preferred to show people what they would gain by following him and what the kingdom of heaven is like.

Introducing Jesus as our light in this dark world gives our friends something to ponder, allowing a guarded heart to give Jesus another look and freeing people to see Jesus as a promise instead of a threat.

Introducing people to God by threatening them with an everlasting hell may simply encourage people to "accept" Jesus out of fear, or it might make them reject God before they've had time to know him and trust him with their "hell questions." How much better it is to know Jesus first and then wrestle with him about hell![*l*]

If you're talking to a person who says hell is their main reason for rejecting Jesus, consider sharing something like, "I don't follow Jesus because I'm afraid of hell. I follow him because with him my life makes sense." Introducing Jesus as our light in this dark world gives our friends something to ponder, allowing a guarded heart to

---

[*l*] Matthew 25:41.

give Jesus another look and freeing people to see Jesus as a promise instead of a threat.

Knowing Jesus gives our lives meaning before *and* after death. For his sake, let's not make mountains out of molehills.

Chapter 11

Molehills That Are Mountains

A middle-aged woman came up to our table after a Sunday morning service. She bought our books and then engaged me (Jonalyn) by explaining she no longer attends church regularly: "The elders invited me to join the leadership team a few years back. I loved working as a leader here. But when the new pastor arrived, he had very different ideas about women in leadership. I had counted on the existing elders supporting my work, but eventually I had to step down. The Sunday messages are different now, they're just so ... condescending to women. It's changed the way I see God. I used to believe he cared about women serving with men."

Another woman wrote:

> I am a single woman in leadership. My associate pastor recently told me, in front of the other leaders, "You could be a liability because of your singleness and your looks." I am not ugly. I am forty-four and take care of myself. It stunned me. It hurt. I stumbled out of that ministry. The sad part is, I let it eat away at my confidence. It almost destroyed my desire to serve. I am now taking my gifts into secular recovery where women are more appreciated and respected. Perhaps there I will not feel so stifled?

In our work, we hear more and more stories like these about the heartache of Christian women in this country.[1] Many women have examples of their churches silencing them. One wrote of being warned to "tone it down" before joining a Bible study because her Bible knowledge would intimidate the men. We've heard women tell us they've been belittled, overlooked, or accused of being too attractive or "Jezebels" (i.e., strong personalities).

Today, many women will reject Jesus because they find the secular world valuing their abilities more than their local church.

For decades in America, unmarried women could not expect a vibrant leadership role in the church or the world. But today, many women will reject Jesus because they find the secular world valuing their abilities more than their local church.

We do not suggest dismissing passages in Scripture to make some women happy. But we do suggest reconsidering if we truly understand an issue like women in ministry beyond what our traditional Christian subculture has typically taught.

Topics once preached as the plain meaning of Scripture have become major reasons for people rejecting Jesus, reasons like respect for pastors' authority in spite of glaring hypocrisy, unkindness toward the gay community, and the stunted role of women in the church. We've heard each issue cited by non-Christians as sufficient reason to reject Jesus, his church, and his people. Because we believe that our friends have not rejected Jesus, but rather rejected a particular version of Christianity, we've been studying how to talk about these topics in a helpful, biblical, loving manner.

We can all share our convictions and well-researched beliefs, but when it comes to any nonessential doctrine—and there are *far* fewer essential doctrines than we like to think—we must preface our beliefs with, "This is what I believe the Bible teaches, but followers of Jesus disagree about this issue. I think we have freedom to believe differently and still be followers of Jesus."

Then we need to live with love what we believe to be true.

Why Are There So Many Hypocrites in the Church?

The hypocrisy in the Christian church is a serious barrier to people who might otherwise seek Jesus. While there are many Christians who follow Jesus closely and faithfully, our whole religion loses credibility when those who claim to love God live like God's enemies.

A hypocrite isn't just any person who makes mistakes, but someone who publicly decries a sin while practicing it privately or enabling it. Consider an author who writes that husbands should love their wives—but he verbally abuses his wife. Or the Bible study leader who tells his group that Christians ought to love Mormons—only to mock them moments later for holding "crazy beliefs."[2] Think of church leaders who preach about "saving marriage" from the attacks of homosexuals while sanctioning divorce and remarriage within their congregations. Or the Christian youth leader who teaches about God's universal love but talks about "retards" and "homos" before the Wednesday night service.

Even the most tolerant person cannot tolerate hypocrisy, especially from religious people.

As we've seen in today's culture, even the most tolerant person cannot tolerate hypocrisy, especially from religious people.

We all live with some measure of hypocrisy, conscious or unconscious. The problem we're specifically facing is that Christians are becoming *known* for their hypocrisy.[3] One nonbeliever explains, "You could say I am a lot like Christians—I have gotten good at telling people what I think they want to hear. I see why Christians do it. They want to look good."[4]

Christians struggle with hypocrisy because of our core confusion about what Christianity means. We tend to believe that Christianity is more about being good than about following Jesus.[5] If we believe this, when we try to share our beliefs with others, we talk more about attending church, praying a sinner's prayer, and becoming a good person than about Jesus. The result is that we become known for morality, not for our love of Jesus.

Christians all understand how hypocrisy festers among us. Thousands of years ago, in Paul's first letter to the Corinthians, he writes, "I am writing to you that you must *We become known for* not associate with any who *claim to be fel-* *morality, not for our* *low believers* but are sexually immoral or *love of Jesus.* greedy, idolaters or slanderers, drunkards or swindlers. With such persons do not even eat."[a] Paul is not forbidding friendships with unbelieving sexually immoral, greedy, idolatrous, slandering, drunk, swindler types. He only forbids such friendships with these people *if they claim to follow Jesus.* As Paul puts it, "What business is it of mine to judge those outside the church? Are you not to judge those inside?"[b] What a helpful verse for these times!

Paul tells us to judge those in the church. If the church is full of hypocrites, are we confronting them? Such loving confrontation must always begin with a confession of our own hypocrisy to pave the way. If we have prayed and approached our brother or sister in love, the result is usually healing. Such rebukes can jump-start our idling lives with God, reminding us that we can be fully known and loved.

Surprisingly, our moral behavior can actually hide us from the God we claim to serve. Jesus tells us we will know his followers by their fruits, not by their moralisms—church membership, strict attendance, Bible-reading plans, parochial schools, or large donations. Moralism offers the tempting double advantage of giving us a flawless veneer and the subtle smugness that we've worked our way into God's favor. Spiritual director John Coe writes:

> From the ancient sages to Aristotle to the modern moralist, the project of morality and the claim that 'I am good, I am moral' has been the most used defense as a way to hide from

---

[a] 1 Corinthians 5:11, emphasis added.   [b] 1 Corinthians 5:12.

God and the need for a Savior. It has been this way from the beginning, since our first parents.[6]

Paul lists the fruit of God's Spirit to test those who know him.[c] Paul's list stands against the endless lists of social standards we prop up to look like "Christians." These qualities—love, joy, peace, patience, kindness, goodness, faithfulness, gentleness, and self-control—are impossible to consistently mimic by rule keeping. The fruit of the Spirit creates a flexible, creative life flowing only from true apprentices of Jesus as works of art flow from the brush of a master artist.

When friends of ours tell us that all Christians are hypocrites, we give them this short list of spiritual fruit. "You're right that hypocrisy is a problem," we tell them, "but this is how you spot the real Jesus followers amid the impostors." (Remember Manner #4 on page 43.) A simple statement like this also introduces them to the God of Israel, who wants us to become people who carry God's good presence.

This is how you spot the real Jesus followers amid the impostors.

The fruit of the Spirit grows in communities of openness. Hypocrisy thrives in the environment of closed doors and buried secrets. When people hide their true selves, they, in turn, prevent others from being themselves. This cycle of shame disconnects us from each other and God.

When friends of ours find another example of Christian hypocrisy, we often offer another example of our *own* hypocrisy—and how Jesus helped us grow and change because of it. The most disarming way to respond to a charge of say, "Christians act all pure, but they gossip as much as everyone else," is to share how we have gossiped and what helps us change. We can share the Christian practice of confession even as we talk about Jesus. Sharing stories of openness and love serves beautifully to remind our friends that not all Christians live a double life.

---

[c] Galatians 5:22–23.

Frederick Buechner, in his book *Telling Secrets*, notes that churches would do better to function like AA meetings than like country clubs. Instead of repeating the often oversimplified story of the salvation message, instead of sitting passively in our seats while a few on the stage lead us through the one-hour program each Sunday, what would it be like if we peeled off our layers and engaged one another by asking for help with the regular sin in our lives? Do others know who we are? Do they know how we struggle? Do we take the initial steps to let people know where we stand? For instance, do our fellow Christian friends know if we're in therapy, if we've had a miscarriage, if we struggle with an irrational phobia? Who really knows us?

What would it be like if we peeled off our layers and engaged one another by asking for help with the regular sin in our lives?

How fascinating church would be to hear each other's secrets and realize we are not alone in ours. How helpful church would be if we regularly heard how Jesus helps us overcome the fear of letting our hidden world pour out into our public world. How unique a perspective the world would see if we were regularly concerned with loving those who fail!

Our fortification against hypocrisy begins with our confession. Confession builds trust, humility, and community. We are all in this together.

How Do I Love My Gay Friends?

Christians have a difficult time loving gay people, and that, by any biblical measure, is a problem. Like the priest who stepped around the beaten man in the parable of the Good Samaritan, we Christians often fail to love neighbors dramatically different from us. This matters a great deal. In our culture, we can no longer pretend that homosexuality is a molehill we can ignore.

Jesus never mentioned homosexuality, but Paul did. We believe that Paul would not list homosexual sex with other sins in the first chapter of Romans unless we needed to take it seriously.[7] However, we are open to our minds being changed and our understanding of Scripture clarified. We maintain friendships with our gay friends, and we pray for the privilege of many more relationships with our homosexual brothers and sisters, both inside the church and out. Out of these friendships we want to share our observations with you.

Our goal here is to share how we talk about Jesus with our gay friends.[8] Having the conversational manners to speak in love is essential. As one gay Christian said, "My wish for the church would be that we would not be homework to them to solve, but that we would be people."[9] If we can recognize every gay friend as a man or woman made in God's image, we can enjoy rich spiritual conversation.

Many of us give little thought to the moment-by-moment experience of gay people. Gay people, like anyone, reach out to hold that which gives them hope and are often afraid to admit they are Christians. Our number-one concern is to humanize our talk about homosexuality so that we can have kind and respectful conversations with our gay friends.

Every gay person we've spoken with knows what the Bible says about homosexuality—and the Christian distaste that often accompanies it.

Gay people find that few, if any, of their Christian friends will stand by them as they come out. This should cause us to pay attention. Every gay person we've spoken with knows what the Bible says about homosexuality—and the Christian distaste that often accompanies it. I (Dale) was writing at a local café when the cashier came over to my table to chat. I asked him his name. "Cornelius," he said.

Surprised by the uniqueness, I asked, "Cornelius? That's a Bible name, isn't it?"

"Yes, that's right, Acts chapter 10."

"I'm impressed. Are you a Christian?"

"Nope, nope." He shook his head. "I'm gay and those two things just don't go together."

Most gay friends of ours have stories of coming out and hearing a Christian "rebuke them in love" or explain to them, "You know that is sin, right?" And all have struggled (and often continue to struggle) with believing that their intimate desires and their sexuality are displeasing to God.

We have learned that no matter what verses you know or how you feel—be it empathy, fear, abhorrence, concern, or anything else—conversing with a gay person is not the time to quote Bible verses. Nor is it about "loving the sinner, hating the sin."[10] This stops conversations cold. Our sexuality is so fundamental to who we are that we cannot treat homosexuality like we treat gossip or pride or anger. When we step into the shoes of a gay person—imagine, if you are heterosexual, being told that your ever-present attraction to the opposite sex is both a choice and a sin—we realize that speaking with grace, humility, and love is the only proper course of action.

Conversing with a gay person is not the time to quote Bible verses.

For everything there is a season, and now is the time for Christians to be tender toward our gay neighbors. If we care about honesty and hate hypocrisy, our very first response needs to be gratitude to any person revealing their homosexuality. They have chosen to be honest with us about something incredibly personal. Let us be quick to thank them for opening their hearts to us.

Second, become a willing listener (Manner #2). Coming-out stories are full of courage and pain. Listening to these stories reminds us that whenever a person shares their stories, it creates community. Our religion is a narrative one, from the patriarchs to the exodus and from the kings to the newborn King. Coming-out narratives remind us that gay people suffer persecution and verbal or physical attacks.

Third, we strive to be open and interested in the ongoing journey of our gay friends. As one of our friends wrote, "Thank you for being open to learning. I take no offense to any questions. The times I find the hardest are when people refuse to listen. I am not trying to make anyone conform or become me. My goal has always been understanding and living equally with others. I wish more people understood that."

To show that we want to create a safe place for our gay friends, we've opened discussions with questions like these:

- Would you be willing to share with me your coming-out story? I'd love to hear it.
- Are you in a committed relationship? How is that going?
- How have your parents responded?
- How do you feel when you hear marriage preached as between one man and one woman?

Finally, after dozens of discussions and dinners and luncheons and phone conversations, we've broached more difficult questions that feel natural and appropriate:

- What do you think of God?
- How have you experienced Jesus?
- Do you struggle with anything you've heard in the Bible?
- Do you think the Bible is outdated?
- Do you believe God forbids gay relationships?

After many conversations, I've (Jonalyn) asked one of my lesbian friends to help me understand how she interprets the biblical passages about homosexuality. Her response is that either these passages are outdated,[d] culturally specific,[e] or aren't talking about homosexuality as it's meant today.[f][11] When she hears these verses quoted, she feels they're often used by people who just want to hate gays. What's sad to us is that Christians often quote verses as an excuse to avoid asking questions and getting to know gay people.

Movies can help us understand what gay people experience. One we can highly recommend for its nonpolitical insights is *Through My Eyes*, a documentary of sincerely straightforward and informal testimonies from young American Christians who are gay

---

[d] Leviticus 18:22.   [e] Romans 1:26–27.   [f] 1 Corinthians 6:9; 1 Timothy 1:10.

or lesbian.[12] The video also contains a four-page discussion guide that provides a simple and effective way to step into the shoes of a gay person without feeling forced to approve or disapprove.

We've learned that we can sound naïve or unkind unintentionally, such as when we assume that heterosexual sex will "cure" a homosexual or when we casually suggest that all gay people simply need to be "healed." But the most important change Jesus followers can make is to refuse to mock homosexuals. Have we ever called someone a "fairy" or made a limp-wrist gesture? When Ellen DeGeneres' show comes on, do we call her "Ellen Degenerate" or exclaim, "Ewww! She's gross"? If we talk about gay people as "just wrong" or "sick" with our inner circle of friends, we can be certain that we will never experience friendship with a gay person—because we still have the residue of a nonloving attitude. More often than not, homosexual friends struggle silently, and our mockery forces them to remain isolated and develop a skewed picture of Jesus.

Any hint of fear or disgust in our eyes or body language tells gay people loud and clear that we do not want to know them. In college, I (Jonalyn) visited a friend's dorm. She had taped a sign to her door that read, "I am against gay bashing." When I raised my eyebrows and questioned her on why she would stand up for gays at all, she turned to me and said, "Jonalyn, I am against anyone harming a person, gay or straight."

We are God's ambassadors, showing the world the way he loves gay people.

I stood corrected.

Standing up for the rights and safety of people with whom we disagree is just and good. Though people without context may assume that since we have gay friends we also endorse all gay sex, gay events, and gay politics, we have to take that risk, caring more deeply about God's reputation of loving others as our neighbors. We are God's ambassadors, showing the world the way he loves gay people. If we are in youth ministry, this means safely welcoming teens who share their same-sex desires and refusing to treat them like a disease. It means not requiring someone to publicly confess their same-sex attraction. We would not require them to leave our youth group for the same reason that we would not ask *any* marginalized teen to leave.

Fourth, avoid the phrase, "The plain meaning of Scripture is ..." because *no one* likes to be patronized. Anyone who has delved into the predestination debate (or women's public ministry, or the end times, or creationism, etc.) knows the "plain meaning of Scripture" is often the "plainest" to us, while Christian experts disagree on all these topics. Do not be tempted to use this phrase as a defensive tactic to keep yourself from having to wrestle with the issue.

Finally, avoid arguing against homosexuality from the Old Testament. The attempt at gang rape in Genesis 19 is not precise enough to be helpful. And later, Ezekiel tells us that the the sin of Sodom and Gomorrah was something other than homosexuality, rather oppression of the poor and stranger: "This was the sin of your sister city of Sodom: she and her suburbs had pride, excess of food, and prosperous ease, but did not help or encourage the poor and needy. They were arrogant and this was abominable in my eyes."[g] Examples in Leviticus, such as the often used "abomination" passage,[h] are also difficult to apply because few, if any, Christians follow the Mosaic Law.[13]

Eventually in all our friendships with our gay friends, they ask us what we think about the biblical passages that speak against same-sex eroticism. In 1 Corinthians 6:9 and 1 Timothy 1:10, homosexuality is listed as one of many wrong acts. Advocates of Christian homosexual relationships explain that the homosexuality in these passages was prostitution or forced sexual liaisons and often involved minors — a far cry from two naturally oriented homosexuals.

While we respectfully listen to this view, we prefer to build our case about homosexuality from Romans 1, in which Paul writes

---

[g] Ezekiel 16:48–49. [h] Leviticus 20:13.

that both men and women who practice homoerotic activity (as well as those who practice greed, envy, murder, strife, deceit, malice, gossip, slander, hatred of God, insolence, pride, and disobedience to parents) are people who do not want to know God. We interpret Paul's words as a warning against homoerotic *behavior*. This has been the position of most Christians for thousands of years long before it became political.

We interpret Paul's words as a warning against homoerotic behavior.

Even as we share our views, we must keep in mind several things:

- Evangelical, heterosexual, biblical scholars disagree over the various homosexual passages in the New Testament.[14]
- Many of our gay friends *do* want to know God.
- Many of our gay friends have their own researched interpretations of Bible texts that we would do well to listen to and research on our own.[15]

If we're discussing Scripture, we must continue to study so we land on a reasonable interpretation that takes context and culture into account, not merely the influences of our own church and culture.

The Bible never condemns a homosexual person for feeling same-sex attraction.

One insight we find helpful is that the Bible never condemns a homosexual person for *feeling* same-sex attraction, a misapprehension that causes needless guilt and shame among a growing number of young people questioning their sexuality. When speaking with youth, we often ask, "Do you think Jesus doesn't love you because you have these feelings?" We want them to feel safe to talk about their desires *while trusting that we and Jesus love them*. With a willingness to listen without leaping to condemn, we can break down doors of secrecy and shame.

Since we personally know gay people who love Jesus, we share their stories with friends who fear their homosexuality keeps them from God. As with any issue, and any person, our goal is to introduce them to Jesus, our mutual friend and teacher.

Is the Bible Sexist?

We formed a circle to pray together in the green room before a speaking event. I (Jonalyn) glanced down and noticed that all the shoes in this circle praying belonged to men. Mine were the only heels in the team of leaders. As we walked out to the auditorium, I smiled because the audience was full of females. We sat down to listen to the opening music. I pulled out my notes and then scanned the team of speakers. I was the only female perspective this audience would hear.

During that conference weekend, wearing my own male shoes among all those male speakers, I (Dale) was discouraged about the sexist language and joking that spilled unaware from Christian leaders. Behind the scenes they reinforced stereotypes that weak men were "girly" and that women made good housekeepers. I don't think they meant to be insulting, yet I saw clear evidence how a man, sensitive to the dignity of women, would resist being part of any group, including a church, that supported and reinforced such views of women.

When we speak as a husband-wife team, I (Jonalyn) regularly meet young women coming out of the shadows to express their amazement that they saw a woman speaking to a mixed audience on the same platform as the men. One fifteen-year-old recently told me, "You're like a big woman with all the men. It makes me think I could do what you do." She made me smile and cringe at the same time. Seeing a woman speak in church is still uncommon enough for a fifteen-year-old to sense a culture shock.

A close friend once confided in me, "Sometimes I think I could get a lot more done in this church if I had a man's body instead of a woman's." As Dan Kimball points out in his book *They Like Jesus But Not the Church*, our culture senses that the church is dominated by males and oppresses females. Though I have not often felt dominated or overshadowed by men, I recognize that our church culture reflects a preference for male leadership. This can be due to personal taste, "I feel uncomfortable with a woman preacher," or Bible verses, "I do not permit a woman to teach or to assume authority over a man."[i]

While I can point to Christian men in my life who value my input, my mind, and my leadership, their support does not erase the experiences of men telling me that I have no place in sharing reflections or preaching on Sunday morning or even working on a theological book. Dale and I have both been discounted and shunned because we believe women are created to partner with men in all aspects of life and ministry. Whether you agree or not, all Christians are called to value women equally to men, as Jesus did, as God did when he made man and woman.

All Christians are called to value women equally to men, as Jesus did, as God did when he made man and woman.

The body of God functions best when both men and women can assist each other in serving the community. As men currently shoulder most of the visible leadership, we notice the gaping needs regularly. I (Jonalyn) recall what a teenager recently told me after we spoke to their youth group: "I haven't been able to talk about it [sexual abuse]. All the youth pastors are men, and I just don't feel comfortable asking them my questions. I'm tired of feeling afraid of men. I just want to know if God will take that away from me..."

The visible leaders in most of our churches are men, and this, regardless of what we believe about women in top leadership, can lead modern Americans to the conclusion that God might prefer men to women. Women who read the Bible might think that the God of Israel prefers males to females. Throughout the Hebrew Scriptures most of the animals sacrificed in the temple were male,

---

[i] 1 Timothy 2:12.

the priests were male, and the leaders (prophets, priests, kings) were almost exclusively male. Women are punished with pain in childbirth;[j] judged to be ruled by men;[k] relegated as weak;[l] silenced;[m] barred from teaching;" and instructed to call their husbands "Lord."[o] Even this abridged list is daunting. How can we answer the charge that the Bible, and not simply the American church, devalues women?[16]

We believe that the Bible, when read properly, offers much more freedom than our churches admit—a freedom that sounds like good news to many of our friends, both in today's culture and inside the evangelical church.

When friends of ours ask us to weigh in on the big gender passages like 1 Timothy 2 or Ephesians 5, we explain how scholarly Christians disagree about these passages before explaining our view: equality and partnership in marriage and church roles.[17] Regardless, we encourage our friends to look at the Scriptures themselves, read in context with the rules of genre. We want them to see how many times God uses women to lead with men.

Women in the Bible

God created woman to reflect his image[p] as helper.[q] The Hebrew word for helper, *ezer* (pronounced *a-zer* as in "razor"), is also used to describe God. *Ezer* means the protecting, sustaining help that God gives, not merely an "assistant." *Helper* is also the name Jesus gives to the Holy Spirit. From the beginning, God had good plans for women.

Throughout Scripture, the God of Israel places strong women alongside strong men to help accomplish his purposes, women like Ruth and Abigail and Esther. During King Josiah's reign, the male priest and male advisers consult a female prophetess to validate the Book of the Law.[r] Josiah says, "Go and inquire of the Lord for me

---

[j] Genesis 3:16. [k] Genesis 3:16. [l] 1 Peter 3:7. [m] 1 Corinthians 14:34. [n] 1 Timothy 2:11–15. [o] 1 Peter 3:6. [p] Genesis 1:27. [q] Genesis 2:18 and 20. [r] 2 Kings 22:14–20 and 2 Chronicles 34:14–33.

about what is written in this book that has been found."*s* Huldah appears to be the king's first choice for discerning God's direction.*t* Her words authenticate the long-overlooked Torah and propel King Josiah to renew Israel's covenant with God.*u* In all these examples, we note the presence of godly women in an ancient, patriarchal culture, an observation that seems to suggest that limitations on women are more often created by men than by the God of Israel.

If God only approves of men in positions of leadership, what do we make of Huldah, or the judge Deborah, or the husband-

Jesus, who, more than any other ancient religious teacher, recognized, respected, and empowered women.

wife team of Priscilla and Aquila who instruct Apollos about his doctrine?*v* Did these women simply disobey God's appointed order when they spoke up? Or were they following and serving God just as any man is called to do? Based on the fruit of their leadership, and on Jesus' interactions with women, we believe the latter.

Along our journey, the most helpful answer we can give those who find sexism in the Bible is to introduce them to Jesus, who, more than any other ancient religious teacher, recognized, respected, and empowered women. In 1873, Reverend Thomas Webster wrote *Woman: Man's Equal*. The opening line begins, "Christianity is the special friend of women ... This elevation is the natural outgrowth of the example and teaching of Jesus of Nazareth."[18]

We love bringing up Webster's point today.

Buddha, Muhammad, Jesus, and Women

In ancient times, men, even religious founders, exploited females or ignored them altogether. Muhammad (AD 570–632) assisted women sporadically, depending on his needs and revelations from Allah. He began his spiritual journey with a powerful woman, Khadija, at his side. But once Khadija died, Muhammad married

---

s 2 Kings 22:13.   *t* 2 Kings 22:14.   *u* 2 Kings 23:2–8.   *v* Acts 18:24–26.

many women. He ended the practice of female infanticide, but he also taught that husbands should beat disobedient wives,[w] calling women "snares of the devil.... Put women in an inferior position since God has done so."[19]

Siddhartha Gautama, later known as the Buddha (563–483 BC), initially excluded women from following his teaching, thinking women were incapable of paying the price of a monastic life, even teaching that women could never become Fully Enlightened.[20] Only after his stepmother shaved her head and proved her endurance did Buddha change his mind.[21]

Despite the fantasies of conspiracy theorists like Dan Brown, Jesus neither married nor excluded women from his teaching. He ate and traveled with women who cared for his needs.[x] He protected women and widows through individual miracles,[y] teaching in women's favor,[z] interpreting the Law's meaning for their benefit,[a] and noticing them even when they were marginalized.[b] From Jesus' conversations with women, we learn that he trusted them with vital teachings such as, "God is spirit, and his worshipers must worship in the Spirit and in truth"[c] and "I am the resurrection and the life."[d]

> *Jesus had faith in women, welcoming their questions and engagement.*

Jesus had faith in women, welcoming their questions and engagement. He permits Mary to stay near him and learn along with the disciples.[e] He commands Mary Magdalene to preach the good news: "Go to my brothers and tell them, 'I am ascending to my Father and your Father, to my God and your God.'"[f]

Thousands of years later, Simone de Beauvoir, the brilliant French existentialist, atheist, and feminist, admitted it was Jesus and not modernity that first set women free. She wrote, "It was Christianity ... that was to proclaim, on a certain plane, the equality of

---

[w] Qur'an 4:34.   [x] Mark 15:40–41.   [y] Mark 5:25–34.   [z] Mark 12:38–40.   [a] Mark 14:6–9, Matthew 19:3–9.   [b] Mark 12:41–44.   [c] John 4:24.   [d] John 11:25.   [e] Luke 10:38–42.   [f] John 20:17.

man and woman ... she is God's creature, redeemed by the Saviour, no less than is man: she takes her place beside the men."[22]

During a women's retreat last year in Seattle, I (Jonalyn) had a long conversation with a woman who was spiritual but not religious. She told me she had come to the retreat to get some information about spirituality as she was writing a new book. As we pressed into questions of identity and womanhood that weekend, she'd come up afterward to talk more. Our conversations deepened. Later the next day she said, "I'm really liking what you're sharing about the Bible. I don't know anything about it, but you make me want to read it more."

The next morning, after talking about how Jesus uniquely loves and frees women, she gave me two thumbs up.[23] In our last conversation she told me, "If this is what God does," she gestured toward all of us women standing around her, "I want more of this."

She met Jesus as a champion of women, not a harbinger of more sexism. As a modern woman herself, she welcomed the way Jesus, not the world, takes the lead in loving and valuing women. This mountain doesn't need to become an obstacle for women, or men, coming to Jesus. The women issue can be a platform for us to share how Jesus shines.[24]

When Jonalyn and I share the pulpit, we inevitably get men and women thanking us for showing us how men and women can lead together. Even churches that will not allow a woman to pastor permit women like Elisabeth Elliot, Joni Eareckson Tada, or Anne Graham Lotz to speak at special events. If these women have something to share, we think all gifted women are eligible.[25]

We believe every Christian ought to value women as much as men are valued.

Regardless of your view about women in top leadership, we believe every Christian ought to value women as much as men are valued. We need to include women in more visible ways. If the pulpit is the center of your church, invite women to share from their lives and thereby show the congregation that you value women's voices as much as men's.[g]

Why Do Christians Abuse Power?

Through our travels and through the emails we receive, we repeatedly hear stories of people leaving their local churches, wanting nothing to do with organized religion, becoming atheists, Buddhists, and of designing their own spirituality. For many, their local church left them feeling stuck between endorsing the vision of the leadership or feeling excluded.

Serena, a middle-aged member of a small Bible church, attended a meeting to discuss the new pastor's leadership proposals. She learned about a new church policy requiring all congregants to sign a renewed membership agreement, proving their dedication to the church and promising not to criticize the leadership. Serena expressed her concern. "What would signing a membership paper prove? My friends know I'm committed to Jesus and this church; I will be here regardless." Others agreed with her.

The next week, the new pastor preached about a certain group of *Serena's experience has a name, spiritual abuse, which is often mistaken for good leadership.* "rebellious" people who were attacking God's anointed leadership. Serena was rebuked privately and told that unless she signed the membership document, she would not be permitted to continue leading her small group.[26]

Serena's experience has a name, *spiritual abuse*, which is often mistaken for good leadership. Spiritual abuse, as therapist and former pastor Jeff VanVonderen explains, "occurs when someone in a position of spiritual authority ... misuses that authority [by] placing themselves over God's people to control, coerce, or manipulate them for seemingly godly purposes, which are really their own."[27]

---

[g] Colossians 1:18 and 2:10.

I (Dale) unknowingly enrolled in a spiritually abusive college because I thought this conservative Christian college would help me grow spiritually. I quickly learned that following rules "proved" my commitment to God. The spiritual directors of the hall regularly claimed their authority from God, quoting Romans 13:1–5, meaning that unless they were asking you to do something explicitly immoral, then God's will required absolute obedience. I began to believe God put them in my life to teach me something. They certainly tried, instructing me about God's holy and unbending will for everything: my clothing, my friends, my "devotions," my books, my music, my church, my vocation, ministry opportunities, and even my behavior over summer break. Day after day they modeled to me that the more completely I obeyed the rules, the more spiritually mature I was. While attending this college, I began to see the Bible as an exacting rule book, written to justify southern, Bible-belt moralisms from 1920s Baptist subculture. My highest motivation was fear — hoping to please God by avoiding demerits and scorn from "God's authority."

Just like those who have been sexually abused have twisted views about sex; those who have been spiritually abused often have twisted views about God.

Spiritual abuse is tragic because, like any abuse, it comes out of people who are most likely acting out of the abuse they received; they are perpetuating views about the only Jesus they know. Just like those who have been sexually abused have twisted views about sex; those who have been spiritually abused often have twisted views about God. Spiritual abuse doesn't just exist in small Bible colleges. According to a recent Barna survey, a large majority of evangelical Christians and church leaders measure their own spiritual maturity by rule keeping, rather than by the fruit of the Spirit.[28] This same majority of church leaders also believe themselves to be spiritually healthy and satisfied. In other words, most Christians in ministry feel satisfied to measure their spirituality by making, enforcing, and keeping rules. Rule-keeping institutions draw rule-keeping people.[29] It's no wonder Christians can lead or attend church for decades but remain relationally toxic and emotionally stunted. Our culture sees Christians as rule-obsessed prisoners.

A young teen friend of ours, Tina, had struggled for years with guilt about her same-sex attraction, hiding it from nearly everyone. When she vulnerably confessed this to her youth pastor, he refused to allow her to attend until she publicly confessed her sin to the youth group. Tina didn't know this was spiritual abuse. She just stopped attending and took a nose dive into a promiscuous lesbian lifestyle. When I (Jonalyn) told her I did not agree with how her youth pastor handled her confession, she was overwhelmed with gratitude and disbelief. She wanted to know why. I explained that whenever a person uses threats of shame to maintain control, they are being spiritually abusive. Tina and I continue to talk, but she has not gone back to church.

When a spiritual leader uses superior knowledge, credentials, or power to control or limit another person's intimacy with Jesus, that leadership is spiritually abusive. In the New Testament, a true leader is like a servant, acting in love and confessing their own weakness. Gordon Fee says, "The first and most important task of a pastor is to care. Leaders are acknowledged not for who they are, but for what they do."[30]

All of us are leaders, especially when we volunteer to teach children. Consider the Sunday school ditty, "O Be Careful Little Eyes What You See," a song that tells how the "Father up above is looking down in love." However, the song's real message is that this Father is watching for misbehavior like a sin-sniffing heavenly hawk.[31] Another children's song says, "I am so glad that Jesus loves me, Jesus loves even me." *Even* me? What is so wrong with me that God loves *even* me?[32] Aren't we all broken and fallen?

> When a spiritual leader uses superior knowledge, credentials, or power to control or limit another person's intimacy with Jesus, that leadership is spiritually abusive.

Why do we think we must punish ourselves with more guilt about our sinfulness? Do we flagellate ourselves so God doesn't need to?

We've had conversations with friends who have endured abusive spiritual authority in the church and now keep miles away from any organized religion. The organization wasn't the problem, but when abuse becomes organized, its abuse grows exponentially. Abusive leadership trained many of them to hide their struggles. Told to get in line, accused of disloyalty, isolated, and rejected, some of our friends turned toward other religions, militant atheism, or promiscuity because these at least offered them, by comparison, a chance for honesty and hope. When drugs or casual sex offer more hope and peace than a community of people who claim to love Jesus, the church must confess that something is wrong.

When drugs or casual sex offer more hope and peace than a community of people who claim to love Jesus, the church must confess that something is wrong.

We believe the best way to protect the reputation of Jesus is refusing to grant spiritually abusive people power in our lives. Before abuse happens, we must be aware of what it looks like. It festers most easily in circles priding themselves on being *conservative* (though being *conservative* is usually not the root problem). Read some books about how the abuse works and what to do about it.[33]

Sometimes, to stop the power of abusive people, we need to speak to them privately, while other times we will need to publicly reveal a leader's manipulation. Such criticism must flow from the love and courage in our hearts, not from bitterness or a desire for revenge. Standing against abuse will likely cause additional pain and rejection, which is why most stay silent. But silence kills, hurting the abuser, the abused, and God's reputation. Unless we speak up, the toxins will remain and the world will see a different Jesus than the one on the pages of Scripture.

Even with spiritually abusive people, we want to be quicker to show love than to point out sin. Scripture deeply affirms that value and love are laced into humans through and through, regardless of our brokenness. We are fearfully and wonderfully made, but not many of us have learned that lesson well.[b] Whenever we turn our conversation toward God's delight in humans, we help undo the damage of spiritual abuse.

In talking about spiritual abuse with those who do not follow Jesus, we've found it helpful to point out how abuse is a problem across religions. At a college, during an open forum, one female student interrupted our talk with a common objection: "Being a Christian must be hard—you have to carry the baggage of hundreds of years of church abuses!"

"Actually, being a Christian isn't much harder than any other belief system," I (Dale) replied. "Atheistic dictators abused people and so have sophisticated democracies. It's not a religious problem. It's a *human* problem."

"Yeah, that's right," she said, leaning back in her chair. "Humans abuse a *lot* of things." Humans in the church are no exception.

An agnostic friend of ours recently told us, "It's amazing that you guys haven't disowned your faith. I've got lots of friends who've been though horrible stuff at church, but they don't want anything to do with God."

"I don't want to reject God because people abuse his authority," I (Jonalyn) said. "Humans always abuse things. But I still don't want to judge a thing by its abuse."

As we know Jesus better, the differences between followers of God and those who abuse in his name become clearer. The fruit of the Spirit reveals to us where God is working and who we should trust. And sharing a humble, open walk with Jesus protects us from becoming abusers ourselves.[i]

As we identify abuses in the church we address the power abuse has in our lives. We grow healthy. And this mountain, which keeps many from Jesus, will diminish.

---

[b] Psalm 139:14.   [i] See "Hope for Human Healing" on page 148.

Chapter 12

God Talk

Despite the thin secularism in our culture, conversations about the soul are everywhere.[a] Coffee drinks promise to "warm our soul," perhaps while we eat Ben and Jerry's "Body and Soul" ice cream. Bath and body products ensure we will soothe our soul, and vacations offer practices to renew our souls. But in our conversations we've discovered most people don't know what the soul is.

One evening after a youth event, a teenage student asked, "If only our souls go to heaven, how do we know we're even there?" For her, like most people, our souls don't seem quite as real as our bodies. What good was a soul you can't touch or see? How could something like a soul help us once we're dead?

In our world surrounded by science and technology, visual entertainment, and body therapy, the idea that we have an invisible soul eludes us, like Peter Pan's shadow. And Christians do not all agree. Some Christian philosophers, such as Nancey Murphy and Kevin Corcoran, do not believe in the soul.[1] Often Christians disagree as to the nature of the soul, some believing it emerges out of a human body, others arguing that the soul is an essential part of being human. Many Christians hesitate to use soul language altogether since the soul unduly, to their minds, carves humans into spiritual and material parts. They want nothing to do with the harmful duality that has denigrated the body as evil and the spirit as pure and good.

Yet since Jesus talked so much about the soul, and since our culture is rekindling a love affair with soul talk, we have found that

[a] See "thin secularism" on page 138.

the soul offers us a captivating way to talk about God and his existence.[2] We follow in the philosophy of the Christian philosophers Richard Swinburne, professor at Oxford; Dallas Willard, professor at the University of Southern California; and J. P. Moreland, professor at Biola University, when we defend the existence and potency of the human soul.[3] We believe humans are whole, body-soul beings whose souls survive death but are incomplete without a body. We're convinced that God cares about humans, body and soul, and that he wants us to care about defending both aspects of our humanity.

On a recent plane trip, I (Jonalyn) found myself next to a tall man, Ivan, restlessly trying to find leg room. We struck up a pleasant conversation. After a lull in our small talk, I dragged out my laptop and Ivan returned to his airline magazine.

Engrossed in my book about the feminine soul, several minutes passed before I felt someone watching. My train of thought vanished as Ivan broke in, "What are you working on?"

"It's a writing project on women." I didn't look over, hoping to get my thought back.

"Really? What about women?"

"Well ..." I paused. "It's about the woman's soul." There, I thought, nice and succinct. He put his magazine down and turned to me. I felt his eyes reading my screen.

We have found that the soul offers us a captivating way to talk about God and his existence.

"You're serious?" he asked. When I nodded, he looked at me like I had sprouted two heads.

"How can you write about something that doesn't exist?"

"What makes you think it doesn't exist?" I responded.

"Because it's invisible, and invisible things don't exist." He wasn't challenging me; he was merely stating a fact. I checked my watch.

"Ivan, can you give me a few minutes? I'd like to show you that the soul exists." He looked incredulous. Down went his magazine. I began with a simple question, "Do you remember your mom being a good mother?"

"Yes."

"How do you know?"

"She was always there for me." He paused, "At night she'd read me stories."

"So you believe that your mom loved you?"

Ivan nodded.

"Okay, let's do a thought experiment. Imagine you go into surgery and a scientist takes every cell in your body and examines each cell carefully with a powerful microscope. Even if the scientist has a lot of time, will he find your belief, 'My mother loves me' in any of your cells?"

"What do you mean?"

"Where is your belief, 'My mother loves me'?"

"In my brain."

"Okay, so the scientist is looking at all your brain cells; where will he find the belief?"

"I don't know, don't scientists ..." He stopped midsentence. "Brain surgeons know how to detect thoughts and beliefs in our brains ... they just look inside the brain ..."

"And they find our beliefs?"

"Yeah," he was growing less certain. "Don't they?"

"I think they'd find brain activity, but I don't think they'd find your belief that your mother loves you."

"Why?"

"First, because even if a scientist found a belief center in your brain, the stuff holding the belief would be made up of many different pieces, lots of separate material parts. But your belief doesn't feel like it's disjointed by different parts. You even said, 'I believe my mother loves me.' You have an experience of unity, not a bunch of cells or organs in your brain, but *you* believe. Your mother's love is not the same as," I pointed to his head, "the firing of a brain fiber. But there's another reason I don't think scientists will find your belief in your brain ... beliefs are not material."

"So they don't exist!" Ivan responded.

"But don't you believe your mom loved you?"

"Of course."

"But what if scientists can't find that belief in your brain?"

Ivan was sure: "But I know I believe it."

"Then you've got a problem. I think you have three options. If you don't believe in the immaterial world, you either have to keep hunting for something in your brain that can hold all your beliefs, or you have to give up your certainty that you have beliefs, since scientists have not found beliefs like 'My mother loves me.' Or you have to believe that immaterial things, like beliefs, exist.

The conversation about an immaterial soul opened the door to talk about an immaterial God.

"My view is that beliefs aren't material. I mean you can't boil beliefs in a test tube or make them appear in a brain scan. Even if they found a brain region we use for beliefs, scientists could never explain how all that brain activity is the same as the belief 'My mother loves me.' Hormones and synapses can't communicate complex content." I paused.

"I think there is something in you and me, something immaterial, that *owns* all your beliefs."

Ivan sat still, thinking. After a long pause he said, "I bet you're going to tell me it's the soul."

"Yep!"

He leaned back with a sigh. Resting his head back on the chair, he looked over at me. "You sure know your stuff!"

I grinned and told him I had a graduate degree in philosophy.[4] Ivan asked me a few questions and then launched into questions about God. He wanted to know how God dealt with pain, how we could be free but God still know everything. I hadn't even mentioned God, but the conversation about an immaterial soul opened the door to talk about an immaterial God.

We talked for several hours, our computer and magazine forgotten for the rest of the flight. By the time we landed in Los Angeles, Ivan believed in the immaterial world.

Unpacking the Soul

The Hebrews called the life force in God the soul (*nephesh*, e.g., Judges 10:16) or Spirit (*ruach*, e.g., Gen. 1:2) of God. The fact that we are alive is a mark that we came from God. "Then the Lord God formed man of dust from the ground, and breathed into his nostrils the breath of life; and man became a living being."[b]

Our souls are a limited, human version of God's soul, holding our beliefs, feelings, emotions, choices. We don't need our bodies to think or choose, just as God does not need a body (or brain) to think or choose.

While there are many powerful, complicated arguments for God's existence, the evidence for the human soul that I (Jonalyn) shared with Ivan is perhaps the most appealing one we've found. In today's climate, in an everyday conversation, we believe the argument for the soul is an unexpected way to introduce God. Most of our friends already suspect there is a soul, in some sense—they just need evidence to build their faith.

For those less reluctant to talk about spiritual things, the soul is a great way to introduce the reality of the unseen world. Once you can argue for the existence of human souls, then you can move to other immaterial things. After all, if immaterial souls exist, other immaterial things may be out there too.

Who Do You Pray To?

I (Jonalyn) was in a dentist chair, my back molar being outfitted for a new crown, when I began to talk (if you could call it that) with my new dentist. Curt used to attend Hollywood Presbyterian, but he had recently discovered the Law of Attraction and was telling me how it changed his life. I barely got some "um-hmm's" in as he talked. I tried to focus on what he was saying about his spirituality: Curt referred to God as the Life Force; he loved using the Law of Attraction; he was proselytizing me to join his beliefs.

---

[b] Genesis 2:7.

Once I could speak again, I asked, "Do you pray to the Life Force?"

For a moment Curt looked puzzled. "I meditate. I have these great CDs that have chanting on them. You should listen to them sometime. They help me find my center." I still didn't know if he prayed to the Life Force so I tried again.

"Do you ask the Life Force for help?"

"I visualize what I want to do next, my goal set." He paused, "You know I went to church for a long time, and all those Christians think the same thing." I waited. "Christians think that you just need to 'let go and let God' do everything. They're all letting go of their destiny. I say, '*No* way!' that's not how you make things happen. You have to get out there and do something about it. Get what you want."

I had a hard time not immediately reacting to this broad misunderstanding. In some ways I knew what he meant, because some Christians do talk as if they want God to do everything. But Scripture doesn't mean "let go and let God" in this sense. The Bible says we work hard in cooperation with God.[c] But I didn't take the red-herring bait; instead I got back to my original question that he still hadn't answered.

Curt, like many of our friends, had never been asked to explain what God meant to him—he was working it out while we talked.

"So you don't think the Life Force can help you?"

I wanted to understand what "Life Force" meant to him. The question I kept repeating would help me discover what "God" or "Life Force" meant to him. Was his deity a person or impersonal?[d] Asking him about his God with action verbs like *help, answer,* and *listen* gave me a chance to know. A personal God can "answer"; an impersonal deity cannot. Impersonal things cannot choose to do things like "help" you. Curt, like many of our friends, had never been asked to explain what God meant to him—he was working it

---

[c] Philippians 2:12–13. [d] See "Is God Personal?" on page 132.

out while we talked. This makes it all the more important for us to allow our friends spaces of silence between questions and answers.

Curt and I talked many times about the personhood of God. During each visit to the dentist, he would continue the conversation where we left off. Eventually he told me he thought his Life Force was personal. From there I began asking what kind of personal Life Force this was. Was it he or she? Was he interested in the problems we have on earth? Had he made contact with earth?

In beginning conversations about spirituality, we enjoy talking about prayer because the subject feels comfortable to most people. Try this question out by asking your friends if they pray to God. Most people do, perhaps using different names for God, like Higher Power, Life Force, Energy, or the Goddess. The point remains: they pray, which usually means some form of interaction with God, even simple requests like, "Help me," or, "If you come through for me here, I'll do this for you." Any form of bargaining with God is a type of prayer.

If our friends interact with God through prayer, we have reason to believe their God is personal. Then we can ask more questions like, "Have you experienced God interacting with you?" "Does God have feelings?" "Does God care what we think about him?" "Do you think God decides things for us?" Knowing about their God makes it all the more natural to talk about your God. We can't get more than a few questions into discovering our friends' spirituality without them wanting to know about ours.

Is God a Soul?

I (Jonalyn) met Suzanne at Starbucks. She had recently left Catholicism to dabble in her designed spirituality. She bubbled over about the changes in her soul.

"I've never been so close to God," she said, sipping her steaming mocha. "All my life I guess I thought religion was the only way to be spiritual, but now I see more options. I'm becoming, I don't know, more open-minded? I see how God is at the end of all religions."

"You think the same God is behind all religions?"

"Sure, some people pray to the god within them, other people go to church, and other people do yoga and meditate. It doesn't matter what you do, just so that you feel close to God. Just find what works for you and brings you peace. For me, I've noticed something really cool lately."

"What?"

"Hearts just keep coming to me."

"Hearts?" I asked. "What do you mean?"

"Last week I dripped honey, and it formed a heart on my plate. Then I was on a long run, and some rocks came rolling down the hill, right to my feet. They were shaped like hearts. I took them home to remember." She smiled. "They bring me closer to God, you know, like I feel Someone is watching out for me."

After listening, I felt ready to ask her one of my favorite spiritual questions. "In your experience of God, do you think of God as a person?"

"What do you mean?"

"I mean — do you think God has a life? Can God believe and feel and choose stuff?"

"Well, sure . . . that's why I talk to God all the time as if he were sitting right next to me!"

"So does God care about what you think about him?"

"No," Suzanne said. "God is beyond that."

"How do you know God is beyond that? Doesn't God want us to know who he is?"

"I don't think God can be known."

Take a moment and wrestle with Suzanne's beliefs. She just told me that she knew some things about God, like he was right next to her, that he communicated his love with hearts, and that God does not care about us knowing him. All of these beliefs formed

Suzanne's theology—her beliefs about God. And yet, Suzanne also said that God cannot be known.

Since she had shared honestly with me, I wanted to be honest with her,

"I'm kind of confused. You just said God can't be known, but you know something about him: you know he sends you hearts and loves to hear you pray, right?"

"Well, that's true, but why would God care what we think about him? I think of God as above worrying about that."

"Why *wouldn't* God care what we think? After all, like you said, God is a person, and don't persons care about others knowing about them? You and God sound especially close. I know I want those who are close to me to know the real me, to know if I send them gifts or if I have certain beliefs or feelings. Why *wouldn't* God want to be known for who he is too?"

"I guess God does care," she said. "I think he cares that we all know he is love. And everyone believes that!"

God Is Love

Suzanne's confession gave me a wonderful opportunity to link arms with her. Many spiritual designers believe God is love, but they leave off what makes love possible and wonderful. Based on what we know about loving people, they want to be known, they want to know us and reveal themselves to us. God is the same way. We perceive unloving people as closed, "walled up," or "cold," refusing to let their guard down. Loving and being loved, knowing and being known, are the essence of friendship and what a walk with Jesus is like.

Based on what we know about loving people, they want to be known, they want to know us and reveal themselves to us. God is the same way.

When people say God is love, they often don't realize that humans cannot love God unless God reveals himself. It works like this in human interaction as well; we cannot know each other unless we volunteer to share our secrets. Imagine trying to love a God that closed himself to us, refused to share. Is God pleased or withdrawn? Is thunder a sign of his anger? Is sunshine a sign he approves of our behavior? Does God have multiple personalities or one? What does he do to show his love?

Most people believe God is love, but they haven't realized that a loving God is one who reveals himself.

Most people believe God is love, but they haven't realized that a loving God is one who reveals himself. Consider asking them, "If God is a loving person, do you think he wants to be known? Do you think he wants you to know what he is like?" Sometimes we'll use the analogy of love in marriage. We want to know our spouse, not our idea of our spouse. In the same way, we want to know God, not our idea of God.

What Can We Know about God?

In some of our conversations, spiritual designers refuse that extra step that God wants to be known. Perhaps it makes the God of the universe too invasive; perhaps the idea brings up memories of spiritual abuse or a shame-and-blame Jesus. Perhaps it makes spiritual designers feel obligated to God in the same way they once felt obligated in an unhealthy relationship. We can understand these kinds of fears, especially if they are born from hurts and abuse. We want to listen to them.

In response, we can offer our experience of how the God of Israel has been personal in our lives and share how Jesus has walked alongside us. If our friends have a hard time believing a personal God could be love, take time to discover why a personal God sounds unpleasant to them. Listen closely before thinking about replying.

If God exists, God is either personal or impersonal. Only a few religions claim God is personal (for example, Islam, Judaism, Christianity). Fewer clearly teach that all humans are loved and valued as creatures made in God's image (Judaism and Christianity).

Christianity is the only religion that finds a loving community within God's nature, revealing God as three persons living in one essence of Godhood. The God of Israel is the only God capable of showing love without needing to make an angel or human. He always existed as a loving community.

Christianity is the only religion that finds a loving community within God's nature, revealing God as three persons living in one essence of Godhood.

Talking about the personality of God not only builds on everyone's intuition about God and love, it also follows Jesus' lead. Jesus spoke about God in personal terms. Jesus taught about God as a Father who loves and wants us to love in return.[d] Jesus prayed to his heavenly Father: "I have made you known to them, and will continue to make you known in order that the love you have for me may be in them."[e]

Self-disclosure is integral to God's revelation. In Proverbs, God talks about wanting to be understood, sought and found.[f] In Ezekiel, God repeats one refrain to explain his actions, "that you may *know* that I am the Lord," over seventy times (emphasis added). To Israel, God says, "You will call on me and come and pray to me, and I will listen to you. You will seek me and find me when you seek me with all your heart. I will be found by you."[g]

The God of Israel cares what others think about him. When he came to earth Jesus said, "Now this is eternal life: that they *know you*, the only true God, and Jesus Christ, whom you have sent."[h] The more we know Jesus, and the more we know his actions, the more we can share confidently that the God we serve wants to be known.

When we talk with our friends, we get to show them God is a person who cares about what we think about him. Even if our friends don't want to know this God of Israel, it helps them see that to love God means to get to know God. Our loving friendship will continue to show them who our God really is.

---

[e] Luke 15:11–32. [f] John 17:26. [g] Proverbs 8:17. [h] Jeremiah 29:12–14. [i] John 17:3, emphasis added.

Chapter 13

Talking about the Resurrection

Last summer, I (Dale) went on a Jeeping trip with my friend Ted through a difficult mountain pass. After braving rock obstacles and high mountain tundra, we stopped for lunch alongside a lake. We relived the trek to the top, play by play, swapping stories. Our conversation moved to the quietness of the outdoors, special places that remove us from the day-to-day craziness in the world. Then we happened upon the future and suffering, and I shared about my mother's cancer.

"My mother used to joke, 'I'm not in the mood to have cancer today!'"

Ted laughed, "I don't think any day would be a good day for cancer, or for any other kind of suffering."

"My mom talked a lot about pain in her last few years. I don't know why we have so much of it. When I read the Bible I find some explanations in there, but pain still seems to be everywhere, and more than we need."

"Yes!" Ted said as he bit into his energy bar. "My frustration with most religion is that nobody understands pain. Everyone tries to get rid of it, just like I do. But it's there."

"What do you do with the pain in your life?"

"Meditation works pretty well. I don't have to blame God, because he might not even exist or be in control. So I work it out on my own."

"How is that working for you?" I asked, fiddling my fingers over some pine needles.

"Pretty good—like yesterday, my day was upside down. My boss blamed me for things, and I didn't know how to deal with it. So I took my lunch break to slow down and refocus. I realized that my boss could blame me, but I didn't have to take it. I could let it go without being angry. If I didn't return blame to him, I keep protecting myself. That gave me a positive outlook."

"Totally!" I said. "My mom used to say, 'If it doesn't apply, let it fly.' Not always easy, especially when your job is on the line. Looks like you found a way to manage." I paused, and then asked, "Does meditation help you cope with large suffering, like terminal suffering, or even answer the problem of death, like in my mother's situation?"

"I take it a day at a time. Once death comes, either I'll just disappear or my spirit will become one with the universe. I'll find out when it happens. Your mom had to find her own way, you know?"

"I guess so. But wouldn't it be great if we knew someone who did know? When I was a kid, I regretted that I didn't tell my great-grandmother to try to contact me after she died, so she could tell me what it was like. She was almost 102. And for a while, I was upset at myself for not asking her that favor."

"Well, even if you had asked her, I don't know if she could have. You don't hear of the deceased talking to the living. It's kinda hokey," Ted said.

"Yeah. Then I stumbled on something that I'd heard people talk a lot about, but I hadn't considered in a while."

"Yeah?"

"Did you know the Bible talks about Jesus, who went to the other side and came back to tell us about it?"

"But that's what every religion says," Ted protested. "Buddha shows up in others to help people reach nirvana. And the old mystical religions have dying and rising gods. Besides Jesus is in the same book as stories like Jonah and the whale. How on earth could that happen?"

"Good question. Actually Jonah is in another book from Jesus' story. They're hundreds of years apart, so that's not too big a problem to me. And I'm glad you brought up Buddha. Something I've never been able to understand about him is if he comes as different people, how would we know it's the same person back from the hereafter? But Jesus showed up again as the same guy who died just a few days earlier."

Just because a religion says it's true, doesn't mean it's true.

"Okay, I see that. But you're still getting your facts from the Bible. It's so old and it's been corrupted or at least changed.

"I've got some ideas about that; it's a question I've had. But just a sec, do you think it's even possible for a religion to be more true than another?"

"Maybe. But how would you know? Because a priest just told you so?"

"I'm with you. Just because a religion says it's true, doesn't mean it's true. We could both write all sorts of maxims and practices for others to follow,

"If I was going to invent a story as a power-move to dupe the world, I wouldn't include parts that were embarrassing to me."

but that doesn't mean it's true, like God isn't happy with you if you don't like Jeeping!" We both laughed. "Do you mind if I share something I find interesting?"

"Sure," Ted said.

"If I was going to invent a story as a power-move to dupe the world, I wouldn't include parts that were embarrassing to me. For example, if I wrote a book on how cool I am and why everyone should follow my example, I probably wouldn't include the story of when I stayed at a friend's house, as an adult, and accidentally wet the bed.

"You wet the bed? Ha! Sorry, dude, that's pretty bad."

"For sure!" I laughed. "I couldn't figure out a way to hide it, so I just 'fessed up boldly at the breakfast table. I felt like a five-year-old. But you know, I'm sure I'm not the only one." I glanced at Ted with a smirk to see if he'd admit it.

"Well, I haven't done it. Man, I hope I never do."

"Yeah, but if you do, just know you're not alone in the bed-wetting club!" I said. Ted laughed.

"Okay, back to my point. If I were to write the bed-wetting story in a book next to a bunch of stories about how cool I am, which stories would you think were most true."

"The bed-wetting story."

"Why?"

"Why would you put that in there? It kills your story!"

"Yeah, I think so too! Okay, now let's look at Jesus for a minute."

"Does it say Jesus wet the bed?" Ted joked.

"Ha! Not exactly. But the same principle applies. Some people say the church just made up this story to have power over people. But what if there are embarrassing things in the story that keep people from taking the church seriously?"

"Like what?"

"Like the point man. The leading speaker for the church in the Bible is Peter. That's why the Catholic Church, for example, says Peter was the first pope.

"Oh, yeah, I've heard that," Ted said.

"But Peter isn't a very good example of an upstanding leader in the time of Jesus."

"Isn't he the guy who tried to walk on water?"

"Yeah! But he failed after he took a few steps. He kept slipping in. He also refused three times to be called Jesus' friend when Jesus was being tortured."

"He was probably scared out of his mind. I would have done the same thing."

"Me too. But that's not a good reputation for Peter. At one point he corrected Jesus' plans, and Jesus said to him, 'Get behind me,

Satan.'" I paused and smiled, "If you're going to dupe the world with your holy book, you don't call your leading spokesman 'Satan.'"

Ted smiled but was listening intently. "Yep, that's embarrassing and interesting. And the Popes are all proud of Peter."

"And if the Bible were invented, we see some strange details that you would never put into a book designed to deceive people. The stories of Peter tell us that maybe the Bible wasn't invented after all. But there's a more important moment to look at, to see if it is embarrassing."

"Like what?"

"Like what happened three days after Jesus died. We want to ask whether Jesus knows anything about death and what is on the other side of death? Has he seen it?"

"Okay, right, how would we know he has seen it? Has he sent us signs from heaven, writing it on the sky?" Ted chuckled.

"Even better. He rose from the dead. If the story about his rising from the dead was embarrassing, would you at least consider that maybe it wasn't invented?

"It depends."

"Here's something embarrassing: Look at how people treated women in the ancient world. They were considered to be property — gullible, untrustworthy, subhuman types. Women weren't even allowed to testify in a court of law because their words were considered as useless as a thief's." Ted chuckled, as I continued: "Now, if you're going to trick the world into thinking Jesus rose from the dead, you'd be better off writing in some male professor on a morning stroll who found the tomb, documented it, and told all his colleagues about it at the University of Jerusalem. That's what I would expect from an invented document."

"Yeah, that makes sense." Ted said. "Did they have universities back then?"

"Well, sort of. They could have made up someone from the Jewish court of law. You'd want someone credible discovering the empty tomb, right?"

"I get it. But who found the empty tomb?"

"Women," I said.

"Are you serious?"

"Totally serious. Isn't that peculiar? In all four stories about Jesus rising from the dead, every one of them says that women discovered the empty tomb first.

"And that's embarrassing too. Hmmm, very interesting. I've never heard that before," Ted said.

"Yeah, I hadn't heard of it until recently either," I said. "It helped me because I'm naturally pretty skeptical about miracles. It gave me some interesting evidence that the story might be true."

"So what if it is true? Did Jesus talk about the afterlife?"

"He did. He told us before he died and after he died. He must have known what he was talking about, because he didn't change his teaching about the Scripture, about what God was like. Since he rose from the dead, he must be onto something."

The average conversation can't possibly contain everything we could say, so it makes sense to focus on the key Christian event.

"I need to think about this. I've never thought religious stuff could make sense. I thought you just needed faith," Ted said.

We gathered up our trash and hopped in our driver's seats. The trail home was as fun as the trail up the mountain. Ted didn't bring up Jesus again on the trip. Neither did I. But there's always another mountain to climb.

The Central Fact of our Faith

As we've explained ("Mountains That Are Molehills," page 161), we're easily tempted to follow a red herring and derail from the main point in discussions about God. Archaeology and Jonah and the whale are great topics on their own, but often they keep us away from introducing Jesus. The average conversation can't possibly contain everything we could say, so it makes sense to focus on the key Christian event.

When an opportunity arises to be *specific* about our faith, once we have earned a hearing from our audience, we point directly at the resurrection of Jesus. Out of this story flows our faith for loving and following Jesus. The resurrection comforts us when we lay alone with our thoughts of pain and death. The resurrection speaks to our friends' (and our own) deepest questions.

Paul tells us our faith is meaningless without the Messiah's resurrection.[a] And though many features of the Scriptures can be shown to be accurate through historical data, the resurrection helps listeners see Jesus' life, death, and miracles as something that might have actually happened. The resurrection lets us introduce our friends to Jesus, perhaps for the first time.

Why Talk about the Resurrection?

For anyone we speak with, regardless of age, the resurrection stands out in bold relief, framing Jesus as a one-of-a-kind religious founder. For us, the resurrection means more than heaven. The resurrection of Jesus is the core of our theology, the reason we believe Jesus has the power to make us appropriately human and restore the whole world.

The resurrection shows that Jesus knew what he was talking about. He is an expert on both heaven and earth, the only spokesman we know who has literally lived on both sides of reality, the physical world and the spiritual world, and was able to tell us about it. He not only came from heaven to earth, but after he died, he confirmed it, traveling into the spiritual world and undoing death unlike anyone else. Unlike reincarnation, Jesus returned as the same person, with the same voice, with his personal history intact.

The resurrection verifies Scripture. Since Jesus rose from the dead it shows us that he knows what he's talking about. Therefore, we want to know and follow his views of life and God. Jesus quoted

The resurrection shows that Jesus knew what he was talking about.

---

[a] 1 Corinthians 15:14.

from the Hebrew Scriptures. Because he treated these books as reliable, inspired words from the God of Israel, we do, too. Jesus affirmed that the God of Israel is indeed the true God of the universe. Jesus' resurrection validated his other promise that the Spirit of God would be among his people to help them remember what he had taught them and record this in what we now know as the New Testament.[b] His resurrection proves that God was pleased with him, therefore we count on Jesus as a reliable source of truth as to which holy book to trust.

The resurrection validates human life. God isn't looking to give us an escape from planet earth, but to set things right. Human life seems very good; this is what the God of Israel made humans to enjoy. This earth belongs to the Lord and exists for us to relish the work of our hands.[c] The God of Israel plans to redeem every square inch of our planet that currently groans for renewal, not through systems of government or military might, but through the power of Jesus, who will cure injustice, hunger, painful tears; undo global pollution; and bring peace on the good earth.

Jesus' resurrection removes the sting and fear of death. Jesus defeats the ultimate enemy of human life. Paul talked about the resurrection as the linchpin, affirming every doctrine of our faith, giving us hope that we will never die.[d] Jesus said to Martha, "Anyone who believes in me will live, even though they die."[e] Death frightens us, and understandably so, but we do not need to fear what existence will look like beyond the grave. C. S. Lewis said that when we look into the face of God, we will find ourselves recognizing all we have loved on this earth. He will be as familiar to us as our dearest friend and lover.[1]

Where's the Hope?

My (Dale's) mother passed away a few years ago. She battled cancer for many years and was blasted with nearly a dozen chemotherapies. On her last visit to our home, plugged into an oxygen machine, she

---

[b] John 16:13.   [c] Isaiah 65:22.   [d] 1 Corinthians 15.   [e] John 11:25.

sat at the coffee table with us. She discussed doctors and drugs and next steps. Her body was thin, her skin older than her sixty years. Nothing she conveyed about the doctor's remedies sounded promising. Expecting some new therapy, I asked, "Where's the hope, Mom?"

"The hope?" She put down her coffee cup and looked at me. "The hope, son, is in the resurrection."[2]

Now she is gone. Her body buried in a cemetery in eastern Ohio. But her soul is with God, awaiting a new body to walk out of that cemetery.

We will all die, no matter how expensive or extensive our medical treatments. Our best efforts only prolong life a little. Even poor Lazarus, who experienced a temporary resurrection, had to go through the ugly process of death all over again later.

The deeper the significance of the resurrection penetrates our souls, the more naturally the steady hope of its light will shine in our daily lives.

But the God of Israel offers a permanent resurrection to anyone who longs to be with him. This promise is the ultimate validation of our humanity. If you are a Christian, own this truth. The deeper the significance of the resurrection penetrates our souls, the more naturally the steady hope of its light will shine in our daily lives.[3]

Chapter 14

Happy to Be Human

I (Jonalyn) was in the library browsing videos when suddenly I sniffed something unpleasant. A woman reeking of cigarettes was perusing the shelf directly below me. I stepped away from her. Why couldn't she wait until I was done? Her clothes were rumpled and dirty, and her hair hung in greasy clumps around her face. I felt annoyed, since I was there first—and didn't she know that she smelled bad enough to make people edge away? I thought to myself, "What a mess."

That's when I heard something distinctly from God. "That's what pain smells like."

I glanced back, but the woman was gone. In a split second, the woman became a human again. How could I have thought of her as less? What was her life like? What were her needs? Who was she?

"That's what pain smells like."

We've adapted that lesson in all our conversations. Now, when we are in conversation with people we might tend to avoid, like a teen girl bragging about her sexual exploits, we think, "That's what pain looks like." When we watch as our dinner companions argue, the man cutting off his wife repeatedly to belittle her opinion, Dale's eyes will telegraph, "He's hurting." When we fantasize about one-upping someone in our heads, we'll often hear Jesus say, "You're doing this because you're hurting."

A philosopher friend tells us that when Jesus said to love your neighbor as yourself, he means to love your neighbor because that is who you are. Our humanity inescapably connects us to our neighbor. You and I are wound in a network of community, made of the same material, *humus*, earth. We are made to love those around us; we can identify with those in pain. Any friendship that I (Jonalyn) could have had with the woman at the library disappeared when I thought she was more broken than I.

The only time we have a right to talk with someone and introduce Jesus is when we're certain we see them as equally human, broken, and in pain like us. Don't we know pain? The kind that can make us like this woman, unmotivated to care for our body, hunting for any distraction, sleep or cigarettes or DVDs at the local library?

> *The only time we have a right to talk with someone and introduce Jesus is when we're certain we see them as equally human, broken, and in pain like us.*

But when I objectified her as "such as mess," when we capture a person's entire state as "so lost" or "the needy one," rather than a human like me, we cannot really help them. Until we open up to two-way giving and receiving, our acts of charity, whether they be donating, witnessing, volunteering, dining with an argumentative couple, listening to a troubled teen, or striking up a conversation with a woman at a library, will remain drive-by acts of charity. No relationship will be created. People who are good at loving others don't have to premeditate their kindness, gear up for it as if it were a duty best done quickly and gotten over with.

Most of us do not love others well. We don't naturally approach those different from us with this humble question, "What can they teach me?"

When I (Dale) wanted to help a local photographer who was hard up for money, I decided to buy the camera he had been leasing. I loaned him the camera, telling him to use it like it was his and to get out of debt without paying any rental or replacement fee. He would have one year, and then the camera would return to me. He agreed and kicked his commercial photography business into high gear.

In four months he had climbed out of debt. Upon returning the camera, he told us several things. First, no one had ever put their own money on the line for him. Second, he felt more motivated and loved by our loan than all the encouragement people at the church had been giving him. Finally, he offered his friendship and commitment to us, becoming a trusted friend who has helped us in return.

Whenever we want to help another, we need to consider how they will be helping us too.

This photographer's name is Jeff, and his insights introduced this book. We loaned him a camera for a year, but he has given us much more in return. Friendships with people like Jeff bring us back to the point of all spiritual conversations.[1] Whenever we want to help another, we need to consider how they will be helping us too. Jesus loved in this way, allowing us to participate in his work, calling his disciples his friends. Jeff's love has allowed us to participate in his work, too. Jeff's friendship continues to build us as he teaches us more about what it means to be appropriately human. We learn from him, and he learns from us.

Our hope is that you will find many friends to learn from as you talk about Jesus. We want this book to serve not merely as a collection of apologetic tools, but as a road map guiding you toward freedom to be yourself as you talk about Jesus. We hope you will customize your conversations to the unique gifts God has forged in your soul. May you develop your own questions and ideas to introduce others to the God of Israel. May you continue to be taught and humbled by the humans God places in your life.

One day when I (Jonalyn) was gardening, I noticed our young neighbor sitting on his back porch. I'd already categorized him as "difficult," since all he seemed to care about was beer, television, and the constant stream of women coming and going. On this day, he noticed me and walked over to talk while I gardened.

"We're moving soon," I told him, sharing our plans to relocate.

"Oh, that makes me sad," he said. "I saw all those cars at your house last summer, and I knew you guys were doing a Bible study. I really wanted to come. Will you be doing a Bible study this summer?"

"I hope so," was all I could manage. I had judged him falsely. How had we failed to invite our real neighbor to our neighborhood Bible study? I asked for his phone number so we could let him know our summer Bible study plans at our new address.

Coming inside, I asked Dale why we hadn't thought of including him.

"We didn't expect he would come. Isn't he the one who crashed through our yard last winter without apology?" Dale reminded me. That's true, we had no idea he would be interested. We thought we knew who he was and what he would like. But we never asked.

Now we knew. We had a common interest, something to chat about.

We're glad Jesus wants to make us more appropriately human, because we have plenty of material for him to change.

How often we fail to see our neighbors as potential friends. We're glad Jesus wants to make us more appropriately human, because we have plenty of material for him to change. Looking at each other and this world, we're glad God had the interest to become human and live right in the middle of our mess.

Jesus died to make our humanity a mark of God. Let's not excuse our failure to love our neighbors — "What do you expect, I'm only human!" — but rather ask Jesus to remake these broken parts of our humanity. Let us live in the hope that our broken humanity will be where God works his biggest miracle.

As the sun sets over the valley, our neighbor's TV comes on for the night. We pray for him sitting in the dark, and we pray for ourselves. We're all waiting for the fullness of love. He is coming, as surely as the dawn.

soulation℠
sturdy answers. better souls.

Soulation exists to navigate ideas, stir imaginations and help others become appropriately human.℠

Soulation is led by the husband/wife team of Dale & Jonalyn Fincher. As observers of culture, their speaking schedule takes them throughout North America, engaging audiences to be appropriately human. With backgrounds in the performing arts, literature, history, theology and philosophy, they cast apologetics wider than academic debate, showing others how to be robust and savvy followers of Jesus.

Discuss *Coffee Shop Conversations*
and learn how Soulation can serve you,
online @ **www.soulation.org**

Notes

Introduction: Humble Confidence

1. Anne Lamott, *Traveling Mercies* (New York: First Anchor Books, 1999), 43.

Chapter 1: What Is My Neighbor?

1. Annie Dillard, *An American Childhood* (New York: Harper and Row, 1987), 22.

2. Krista Tippett, *Speaking of Faith* (New York: Random House, 2007), 173–74.

3. Lamott, *Traveling Mercies*, 41.

4. Adapted from David Kinnaman and Gabe Lyons, *Unchristian: What a New Generation Really Thinks About Christianity ... And Why it Matters* (Grand Rapids: Baker, 2008), 203–4.

5. Karen Armstrong, conversation with Krista Tippet, NPR, Tippet, *Speaking of Faith*, 43.

6. Madeleine L'Engle, *Walking on Water: Reflections on Faith and Art* (Wheaton, Ill.: Shaw, 1980), 77.

7. John 1:14; L'Engle, *Walking on Water*, 67.

Chapter 2: Loving Discourse

1. C. S. Lewis, "The Weight of Glory," *The Weight of Glory and Other Addresses* (New York: Collier Books, 1980), 19.

2. The "Hound of Heaven" is a metaphor for God in Francis Thompson's classic poem by the same title.

3. M. Scott Peck, *The Road Less Traveled: A New Psychology of Love, Traditional Values and Spiritual Growth* (New York: Touchstone, 1978), 127–28, emphasis added.

4. Evangelist L. Munhall quoted in *The Fundamentals: A Testimony to the Truth*, ed. R. A. Torrey (Los Angeles: Bible Institute of Los Angeles, 1915).

5. Jonalyn Fincher, *Ruby Slippers: How the Soul of a Woman Brings Her Home* (Grand Rapids: Zondervan, 2007).

6. That story is told in the opening of Dale's book, *Living with Questions* (Grand Rapids: Zondervan, 2007).

Chapter 3: Conversation Stoppers

1. Elizabeth Gilbert, *Eat, Pray, Love* (New York: Penguin Group, 2006), 175.
2. www.skepdic.com/faith.html.
3. 1 John 4:18; Frederick Buechner in *Telling Secrets* (New York: HarperCollins, 1991), 26.
4. Shared with permission.
5. Read more about religious addiction in Matthew Linn, Sheila Fabricant Linn, and Dennis Linn's, *Healing Spiritual Abuse and Religious Addiction* and *Good Goats: Healing Our Image of God* (Mahwah, N.J.: Paulist Press, 1994).
6. For more, see Dale Fincher, *Living with Questions* (Grand Rapids: Zondervan, 2007).
7. Mark 2:1–12.
8. For a helpful picture of how inaccurately we view Jesus, search "Jesus video 3" on youtube.com.
9. 1 John 2:1-2; see also Thomas Hopko on forgiveness in this online interview, http://incommunion.org/articles/previous-issues/older-issues/living-in -communion.
10. If you find yourself struggling with blame and shame, reread the book of Mark or John. Listen to the Bible study we put together on the book of Mark, free online (mark.soulation.org). Read it fresh, as if for the first time, and put yourself in the audience watching Jesus. Then ask God to help you treat others the way Jesus treated them.

Chapter 4: Jesus: The Way, the Truth, and the Good Life

1. Our paraphrase of Matthew 13:45.
2. Eugene Peterson, "Dancing Lessons: Eugene Peterson on Theology and the Rhythms of Life," *Mars Hill Audio Conversation 26* (Charlottesville, Va.: Mars Hill Audio, 2008).
3. Please note that simply because a person identifies themselves as a certain religious follower does not mean we ought to take them as a *bona fide* expert in their religion. They will, however, be an expert about what *they* believe.
4. See www.thebigview.com/buddhism/eightfoldpath.html for more on the Eightfold Path of Buddhism.
5. In Spirit of the Disciplines as quoted from *Devotional Classics*, eds. Richard J. Foster and James Bryan Smith (San Francisco: HarperOne, 1993), 16.
6. Ibid., 16.

Chapter 5: How to Read the Bible

1. Millard J. Erickson, *Christian Theology*, 2nd ed. (Grand Rapids: Baker, 1998), 225.

2. Gordon D. Fee and Douglas Stuart's *How to Read the Bible for All It's Worth* (Grand Rapids: Zondervan, 1993), 136.

3. Miroslav Volf as quoted from a conversation with Krista Tippett, NPR, Tippett, *Speaking of Faith*, 175–76.

4. To listen to the series: www.mark.soulation.org.

5. Listen to this conversation: www.soulation.org/media/Mark1112-Mix .mp3 and www.soulation.org/media/Mark1213-Mix.mp3.

6. For more, see Luke 16:1–13 in context.

7. David Plotz, "Good Book: What I Learned from Reading the Entire Bible" *Slate*, www.slate.com/id/2212616/ (March 3, 2009).

8. Ibid.

9. We've adapted this illustration from Walt Russell's hermeneutics class in Spring 2002.

10. Listen to a 45-minute talk about the rules of different genres, "How to Read the Bible II" at www.soulation.org/genre.

11. Since reading all the Hebrew Scriptures can feel very daunting, we recommend the accessible *From Creation to the Cross* by Albert H Baylis (Grand Rapids: Zondervan, 1996).

12. For a handheld illustrated guide, see *The World Jesus Knew* by Anne Punton (Chicago: Moody, 1996); for an encyclopedia, see *New Illustrated Bible Manners and Customs* by Howard F. Vos (Nashville: Nelson, 1999). We also recommend these deeper guides: *In the Shadow of the Temple: Jewish Influences on Early Christianity* by Oskar Skarsaunne (Downers Grove, Ill.: InterVarsity Academic, 2002) and *The New Testament Environment* by Eduard Lohse (Nashville: Abingdon, 1976), 11–196.

13. Jesus quotes Isaiah 61:1–3 in Luke 4:16–21.

14. For a quick summary, see Fee and Stuart's chapter "The Law(s): Covenant Stipulations for Israel" in *How to Read the Bible for All It's Worth*, 149–164.

15. For an interesting read on the medical reasons behind the Jewish laws, see S. McMillian and David M.D. Stern's, *None of These Diseases: Bible Health Secrets for the 21st Century* (Grand Rapids: Revell, 2000).

16. Fee and Stuart, 166.

17. We consulted *The New Illustrated Bible Manners and Customs* by Howard F. Vos (Nashville: Nelson, 1999) for quick background and outline information.

18. For a deeper explanation of this genre, see Fee and Stuart's *How to Read the Bible for All It's Worth.*

19. Fee and Stuart, 45.

Chapter 6: Lost Words

1. Kathleen Norris, *Amazing Grace: A Vocabulary of Faith* (New York: Riverhead Books, 1999), 169.

2. This is Scott Peck's definition of love in *The Road Less Traveled: A New Psychology of Love, Traditional Values and Spiritual Growth* (New York: Touchstone, 2003). We recommend this seminal work to challenge and bolster your views of real love in your family and friendships.

3. Proverbs 7. Notice how honestly the writer describes illicit sex.

4. Matthew Linn, Sheila Fabricant Linn, and Dennis Linn, *Healing Spiritual Abuse and Religious Addiction* (Mahwah, N.J.: Paulist Press, 1994), 71.

5. This phrase borrowed from M. Scott Peck in *People of the Lie* (New York: Touchstone, 1983).

Chapter 7: Misquoting Jesus

1. Rhonda Byrne, *The Secret* (Hillsboro, Ore.: Beyond Words, 2006), 46.

2. Ibid., 183.

3. Ibid., 47–49.

4. Don Miguel Ruiz, *The Four Agreements* (San Rafael, Calif.: Amber-Allen, 1997), 7.

5. Ibid., 30.

6. Ibid., 137.

7. For Tolle, "ego" doesn't mean a prideful person but refers to our souls, our identity, our personhood.

8. Eckhart Tolle, *New Earth* (New York: Penguin, 2008), 71.

9. This is the meaning of "mind of Christ" in Philippians 2:5.

10. A belief is any idea we hold to be true. We use the phrase "Jesus believed" in our conversations as a gentler way to share what Jesus taught. It helps people see the connection between Jesus as the smartest man who ever lived and our own desire to have the same beliefs he had.

11. Tolle, 79.

12. Read the context around Matthew 16:24–25.

13. To get the context, see how Jesus' audience responded in John 8:58.

14. Tolle, 23.

15. Genesis 3:22: We were intended to live forever in the Garden of Eden on earth eating from the tree of life. Revelation 21: God remakes the world for our dwelling where the City of God comes down to rest on the earth. 1 Corinthians 15: We will resurrect with new literal bodies like Jesus. Jewish and Christian theology have always been rooted into God's intention for the earth, redeeming the world rather than escaping from it.

Chapter 8: One True Religion?

1. Christian de la Huerta, *Coming Out Spiritually: The Next Step* (New York: Putnam, 1999), 48.

2. A concise apologetic guide along these lines is Dean C. Halverson's *The Illustrated Guide to World Religions* (Grand Rapids: Bethany, 2003).

3. www.cbn.com/entertainment/books/RaviZ.aspx.

4. Elizabeth Gilbert, *Eat, Pray, Love* (New York: Penguin, 2006), 13.

5. Ibid.

6. Brahman is the impersonal force who later manifests as Brahma (the Creator), Vishnu (the Preserver), and Siva (the Destroyer). For more, see Halverson *The Illustrated Guide to World Religions*, 88.

7. Deepak Chopra, *The Seven Spiritual Laws of Success* (San Rafael, Calif.: Amber-Allen, 1994), 102.

8. *Namaste* literally means, "I bow to the divinity that dwells within you and dwells within me."

9. Krishna speaking in Ravi Zacharias's *New Birth or Rebirth: Jesus Talks with Krishna* (Colorado Springs: Multnomah, 2008), 56.

10. www.himalayanacademy.com/basics/point/index.html.

11. For more examples of Hindu beliefs, look up "Brahman" on Wikipedia.

12. Surah 19:92, see also 88–93, *The Qur'an*, ed. 13, translated by M.H. Shakir (New York: Tahrike Tarsile Qur'an, 2002).

13. Kenneth L. Woodward, "Leaps of Faith," *The New York Times*, December 21, 2008.

14. Austin Cline's primer on secular thought is online here: http://atheism.about.com/od/secularismseparation/p/Secularism101.htm. Also, search Wikipedia for the entry "secularism" for more reading.

15. The Big Bang, for instance, assumes that the time-space continuum had a beginning. This opens the possibility that Something outside of time-space started the Universe.

16. Woodward, "Leaps of Faith."

Chapter 9: The Hope for Human Healing

1. This is the teaching of the Four Noble Truths: 1. Life means suffering (including pain, misery, sorrow, and unfulfilled desires). 2. The origin of suffering is attachment or desiring things which are impermanent. 3. The cessation of suffering is attainable through eliminating all desire for impermanent things. 4. The path to the cessation of suffering is the Eightfold Path and can be reached by all humans. For more, see www.thebigview.com/buddhism/fourtruths.html.

2. www.himalayanacademy.com/resources/lexicon/.

3. Yajur Veda, Brihadaranyaka Upanishad 4.4.5

4. Read more on www.wicca.com. See also "neopaganism" at religion facts.com.

5. See religionfacts.com; islam101.net; islam.com; also, Qu'ran 7:25.

6. See religionfacts.com for an easy analysis.

7. Bhagavad Gita, Sankhya Yoga 2:22: "Even as man throws off worn-out clothes and puts on others that are new, so does he throws [sic] off worn-out bodies and enters into new ones," www.religiousbook.net/Books/Online_books/Bg/gita_2.html. See also www.hinduwebsite.com/reincarnation.asp.

8. As one of the collections of Buddha's teachings, the Anguttara Nikaya, puts it, "My kamma (i.e., karma or past and present actions) is my only property, kamma is my only heritage, kamma is the only cause of my being, kamma is my only kin, my only protection. Whatever actions I do, good or bad, I shall become their heir."

9. A helpful site that succinctly explains Buddhism: www.thebigview .com/buddhism/index.html; see also religionfacts.com.

10. We are indebted to Jonalyn's aunt, Terri Taylor, for helping us with this metaphor.

11. See Brother Lawrence, *The Practice of the Presence of God* adapted in a practical version by Frank Laubach, *Letters by a Modern Mystic* (Colorado Springs: Purposeful Designs, 2007).

12. To read more about how spiritual formation works we recommend Laubach, *Letters by a Modern Mystic* or Dallas Willard, *The Renovation of the Heart: Putting on the Character of Christ* (Colorado Springs: NavPress, 2002).

13. Mark 14:37–38 *The Message*. Or "The spirit is willing, but the flesh is weak" (Mark 14:37–38 NASB).

14. www.interfaith.org/forum/bono-u2-on-grace-and-10162.html.

15. This is similar to Dallas Willard's view. See *The Renovation of the Heart: Putting on the Character of Christ*.

16. Ask LIVE! Private Archives, Winter 2009, www.soulation.org.

Chapter 10: Mountains That Are Molehills

1. Like a house's foundation, essential doctrines hold up Christianity. They can be found within the Christian creeds, such as The Apostles' Creed. Nonessential doctrines are more like doors and windows; even if we alter them, the house still stands firm.

2. See Zondervan's Counterpoints series for an array of hotly debated Christian ideas.

3. The authentic gospels are Matthew, Mark, Luke, and John. Brown claims these are corrupt. Brown prefers the *Gospel of Mary, Gospel of Thomas, Gospel of Judas, Gospel of Philip*. Scholarship invalidates these named authors as the real authors. Gnostic ideas preyed on the teachings of Jesus, using

similar language to teach their own religion. Today Kabalistic Judaism and Sufi Islam claim Gnostic inspiration.

4. The Hebrew text contains the discrepancy, which is a copyist error. This creates confusion, but not a real contradiction. Seven thousand is the correct number, and modern translations reflect that number in both passages.

5. Read philosophical naturalism's remarkable history in *Moral Darwinism: How We Became Hedonists* by Benjamin Wiker (Downers Grove, Ill.: InterVarsity, 2002).

6. World-renowned scientists like geneticist Theodosius Dobzhansky (see his essay, "Nothing in Biology Makes Sense Except in the Light of Evolution" *American Biology Teacher*, volume 35, pages 125–129, 1973); physicist John Polkinghorn (see his essay, "Shining a Light Where Science and Theology Meet," *The Times*, September 19, 2008); and the president of the Human Genome Project, Dr. Francis Collins [see his book, *The Language of God: A Scientist Presents Evidence for Belief* (New York: Free Press, 2007)] believe God used evolution.

7. Jesus used the word "Gehenna" 11 times, like Matthew 10:28. This was the garbage dump of Jerusalem. For a good explanation, see http://en.wikipedia.org/wiki/Gehenna.

8. John Stott and F. F. Bruce, two prominent evangelical scholars of the twentieth century, believed the Scriptures were open to these alternative views. See http://en.wikipedia.org/wiki/Annihilationism for a quick reference.

9. C. S. Lewis stated this view in *The Problem of Pain* (New York: MacMillan, 1962).

10. M. Scott Peck, *People of the Lie* (New York: Touchstone, 1983), 67.

11. Malcolm Muggeridge alludes to alienation like this in his autobiography, *Chronicles of Wasted Time* (Vancouver, BC: Regent College Publishing, 2006).

Chapter 11: Molehills That Are Mountains

1. http://jonalynfincher.blogspot.com/2008/04/how-can-woman-lead-with-power-and.html.

2. A testimony of Curt, a Mormon, as interviewed in David Kinnaman and Gabe Lyons, *UnChristian: What a New Generation Really Thinks About Christianity ... And Why it Matters* (Grand Rapids: Baker, 2008), 42.

3. For surveyed evidence, see Kinnaman and Lyons, *UnChristian*, 41–66.

4. Kinnaman and Lyons, *UnChristian*, 44.

5. Kinnaman and Lyons, *UnChristian*, 49, 51.

6. John Coe, "Resisting the Temptation of Moral Formation: Opening to Spiritual Formation in the Cross and the Spirit," *The Journal of Spiritual Formation and Soul Care* 1, no. 1 (Spring 2008): 60.

7. For a brief summary, see Edith M. Humphrey, "What God Hath Not Joined," *Christianity Today* 49, no. 9, (September 2004) (see online archives). For other perspectives, see David G. Myers and Letha Dawson Scanzoni, *What God Has Joined Together* (New York: Harper One, 2006); Lewis Smedes, *Sex for Christians* Revised Edition (Grand Rapids: Eerdmans, 1994).

8. Our goal is not to give you our theology of sexuality. You can forge your own. Our endnotes will give you a start for different points of view.

9. *Through My Eyes* (Raleigh, N.C.: GCN, 2009) www.gaychristian.net.

10. "Hate the sin. Love the sinner." Mahatma Ghandi. To understand why this phrase isn't helpful, see chapter 3, "Conversation Stoppers," *Showing Fear or Hatred*.

11. To understand these New Testament passages within their cultural context we recommend William Webb's, *Women, Slaves and Homosexuals: Exploring the Hermeneutics of Cultural Analysis* (Downers Grove, Ill.: InterVarsity, 2001) or the shorter interview by N. T. Wright at www.nationalcatholicreporter.org/word/wright.htm.

12. Justin Lee, *The Gay Christian Network* (Raleigh, N.C.: GCN, 2009), www.gaychristian.net.

13. Yet, even if Christians do not follow the Mosaic law, the end of Leviticus 20 references the people in the land prior to Israel's occupation. These non-Hebrews were also expected to keep the sexual laws. This suggests that sexual purity may be more obvious than our need for God to spell it out, holding us culpable regardless of our following the Mosaic Law.

14. Evangelical biblical scholars who believe in supporting monogamous homosexual couples include Robert G. Rayburn, founding president of Covenant College; Marten Woudstra, who taught Old Testament at Calvin Seminary and served as president of the Evangelical Theological Society; Gerald T. Sheppard, who taught Old Testament both at Fuller Seminary and at Emmanuel College in Canada; Reta Halteman Finger, professor of NT at Messiah College in Pennsylvania; and Christian philosopher Nicholas Wolterstorff of Yale University. Evangelicals who believe the Bible stands against homosexuality include the New Testament scholar N. T. Wright; Associate Professor of New Testament at Pittsburgh Theological Seminary, Robert A. J. Gagnon; Stanley J. Grenz, who was Professor of Theology and Ethics at Carey/Regent College; Professor of New Testament at Heritage Seminary, William J. Webb; and Paul Copan, Chair of philosophy and ethics at Palm Beach Atlantic.

15. We believe any conversations about homosexuality must be aware of evangelical Christians who believe the Bible permits faithful, monogamous, same-sex relationships. For instance, Evangelicals Concerned (EC) has been working to blend Christianity with homosexuality without the political heat associated with this issue. We believe you will grow in sensitivity and aware-

ness by exploring these and similar websites: www.evangelicalsconcerned.
org, www.ecinc.org, and www.gaychristian.net.

16. To develop a better understanding of these verses, see *The IVP Women's Bible Commentary* (Downers Grove, Ill.: InterVarsity, 2002); Robert L.
Saucy and Judith K. TenElshof, *Women and Men in Ministry: A Complementary Perspective* (Chicago: Moody, 2001); and Sarah Sumner, *Men and Women in the Church: Building Consensus on Christian Leadership* (Downers Grove,
Ill.: InterVarsity, 2003).

17. Evangelical scholarship is split down the middle about the women issue. You can find many biblical scholars who advocate women preaching and leading (William Webb, N. T. Wright, Gordon Fee, Alice Mathews, Sarah Sumner) and many biblical scholars who do not (Wayne Grudem, John Piper, D. A. Carson, Dorothy Patterson). For a good presentation of both sides, see *Two Views on Women in Ministry* (Grand Rapids: Zondervan, 2005). For more on our view, see www.soulation.org/library/articles/unmuted.pdf.

18. Rev. Thos. Webster, D.D. *Woman: Man's Equal* (New York: Nelson and Phillips, 1873), introduction by Bishop Simpson, www.gutenberg.org/files/11632/11632.txt.

19. Mishkat 26, 651, as quoted in William E. Phipps, *Muhammad and Jesus: A Comparison of the Prophets and Their Teachings* (New York: Continuum, 1996), 149.

20. While a woman cannot become a Fully Enlightened One (*Samma-Sambuddha*), anyone can become a Brahma, a being beyond the world of sexuality or sensuality. See Dr. Hellmuth Hecker, "Man and Woman in the Teachings of the Buddha," presented by BHIKSHUNI NANDABALA, ZenNun. The article is based exclusively on the *Suttas* of the Pali Canon. See www.geocities.com/zennun12_8/woman_man.html.

21. Ravi Zacharias, *The Lotus and the Cross: Jesus Talks with Buddha* (Sisters, Ore.: Multnomah, 2001), 46.

22. Simone De Beauvoir, *The Second Sex* (New York: Vintage Books, 1989), 731, 170.

23. Hear the talk "Coming Home" at www.soulation.org/librarybrowse.html. Search under "Gender."

24. Read our series of "The Treatment of Women" to see how Jesus outshines Buddha, Muhammad, Joseph Smith, and C. T. Russell at www.soulation.org/librarybrowse.html. Search under "Gender." See also Fincher, *Ruby Slippers* (Grand Rapids: Zondervan, 2007).

25. For an example of a gifted woman explaining how to lead in the church see Nancy Beach, *Gifted to Lead: The Art of Leading as a Woman in the Church* (Grand Rapids: Zondervan, 2008).

26. John Bevere's *The Bait of Satan* (Lake Mary, Fla.: Charisma House, 2004) explains how to let go of offenses when wronged, particularly by church leadership. After being passed around at Serena's church, Bevere's message silenced attendees into thinking that raising concerns and speaking up over injustices and abuses was sinful.

27. Jeff VanVonderen, www.spiritualabuse.com.

28. Barna Group Study, released May 2009, "Many Churchgoers and Faith Leaders Struggle to Define Spiritual Maturity." www.barna.org/barna-update/article/12-faithspirituality/264-many-churchgoers-and-faith-leaders-struggle-to-define-spiritual-maturity.

29. As our psychologist friend pointed out to us, "There is a correlation of people drawn to positions of power." Some professions attract more narcissistic people than others; e.g., police, military, and clergy. Not all rule-keeping cultures are run by narcissists, but rule-keeping attracts these kinds of leaders.

30. Quoted from Gorden Fee's lecture at the 2008 National Pastor's Convention. See Fee's influence in the TNIV's translation of 1 Thessalonians 5:12–24.

31. For a helpful, readable treatment of spiritual abuse with excellent solutions see Jake Colsen, Wayne Jacobsen, Dave Coleman, *So You Don't Want to Go to Church Anymore* (Newbury Park, Calif.: Windblown Media, 2006).

32. Jeff VanVonderen uses this example in *The Subtle Power of Spiritual Abuse* (Minneapolis: Bethany, 1991). We both remembered singing this as children and reflect on how subtly damaging it can be to the undeveloped theology of young minds.

33. We've listed some books in the endnotes in this section. Also see *Healing Spiritual Abuse and Religious Addiction* by Matthew Lynn, Sheila Fabricant Linn, and Dennis Lynn.

Chapter 12: God Talk

1. For more see Kevin J. Corcoran, *Rethinking Human Nature: A Christian Materialist Alternative to the Soul* (Grand Rapids: Baker, 2006); Warren S. Brown, Nancey Murphy, and H. Newton Malony, eds. *Whatever Happened to the Soul?: Scientific and Theological Portraits of Human Nature* (Minneapolis: Fortress Press, 1998); and Joel B. Green and Stuart L. Palmer, eds. *In Search of the Soul: Four Views of the Mind-Body Problem* (Downers Grove, Ill.: InterVarsity, 2005).

2. Matthew 16:26. For a comprehensive look at how the soul and spirit are used in Scripture, see John W. Cooper's *Body, Soul and Life Everlasting: Biblical Anthropology and the Monism-Dualism Debate* (Grand Rapids: Eerdmans, 2000).

3. Richard Swinburne, *The Evolution of the Soul* (Oxford: Clarendon, 1997); Dallas Willard, *The Renovation of the Heart: Putting on the Character of Christ* (Colorado Springs: NavPress, 2002); and J.P. Moreland and Scott B. Rae, *Body and Soul: Human Nature and the Crisis in Ethics* (Downers Grove, Ill.: InterVarsity, 2000). For those interested, we consider ourselves Thomistic dualists, that souls are deeply interlaced into the body rather than just bolted to it as Descartes believed.

4. Materialism, or naturalism, is the belief that only material things exist. For more see chapter 10, "Mountains That Are Molehills," section "What about Evolution?"

Chapter 13: Talking about the Resurrection

1. Read through 1 Corinthians 15 for a long description of what awaits us when we walk out of the cemetery.

2. A version of this story is in Fincher, *Living with Questions*.

3. A great place to start studying research on the resurrection is an easily accessible book, Gary R. Habermas and Michael R. Licona, *The Case for the Resurrection of Jesus* (Grand Rapids: Kregel, 2004). Habermas is one of the leading scholars in the world on the resurrection.

Chapter 14: Happy to Be Human

1. Jeff's photography now captures sacred space around the world. See his work at: www.lefever.com/.

Ruby Slippers

How the Soul of a Woman Brings Her Home

Jonalyn Grace Fincher

Jonalyn Fincher wants to show that women can be both fully human and fully feminine. Traditionally, femininity has been a role women play, a role defined by culture and simplistic sermons. The author encourages women to look at the feminine roles or boxes that pinch their souls: mother, fashion devotee, working wife, intellectual. Does God treat femininity as a role, a curse, or a gift? And when Jesus redeemed women, what was it exactly that he redeemed?

Even after Eden, Fincher points out, God planned to redeem both men and women. But for centuries, women have been taught to devalue the very aspects of their souls that are unique and irreplaceable. Femininity itself runs deeper than aprons, frills, or romance. It begins with feminine souls who are living cameos of the triune God.

In *Ruby Slippers*, Fincher takes a fresh, direct look at the challenges she faced on her search for the feminine soul. She goes step by step through what it means to be a woman and how to cultivate her soul, choosing not to shy away from psychology, theology or personal transparency. In her journey she discovers an understanding of femininity that is timeless and groundbreaking. The roles melt away into something like Dorothy's ruby slippers, something women have always had — the souls to walk today with freedom and femininity.

Available in stores and online!

Living with Questions

Dale Fincher

A practical and personal approach to apologetics for students. How many times has your teacher asked you a question, and you stare blankly at the ceiling, hoping to discover the answer lingering there? It's frustrating when we don't know the answers to the questions we're asked by others, but it can be even more frustrating when we don't know the answers to the questions we are asking ourselves. Have you ever asked one of these questions?

- Does what I think really matter?
- What is truth?
- Is God there?
- Has God spoken?
- Am I important enough?
- Am I good enough?
- What's so great about heaven?

If you've ever wondered about any of these questions, you've come to the right place. In *Living with Questions*, Dale Fincher will help you look at each of these questions in such a way that you'll discover clues, helpful tools, and answers — and what they all mean for your life and your faith. The answers you find will put you on a path to dig deeper and gain confidence in your faith. As Dale addresses the big questions that he's been asked by students across the country, you'll find that you're not alone in your doubt, confusion, or questioning. As you learn to live with questions, even the answers are only steps in the right direction. You'll find how they whet the appetite to go deeper into your purpose on this planet and to discover something big — yet very personal — that's worth living for.

Share Your Thoughts

With the Author: Your comments will be forwarded to the author when you send them to *zauthor@zondervan.com*.

With Zondervan: Submit your review of this book by writing to *zreview@zondervan.com*.

Free Online Resources at

www.zondervan.com

Zondervan AuthorTracker: Be notified whenever your favorite authors publish new books, go on tour, or post an update about what's happening in their lives at www.zondervan.com/authortracker.

Daily Bible Verses and Devotions: Enrich your life with daily Bible verses or devotions that help you start every morning focused on God. Visit www.zondervan.com/newsletters.

Free Email Publications: Sign up for newsletters on Christian living, academic resources, church ministry, fiction, children's resources, and more. Visit www.zondervan.com/newsletters.

Zondervan Bible Search: Find and compare Bible passages in a variety of translations at www.zondervanbiblesearch.com.

Other Benefits: Register yourself to receive online benefits like coupons and special offers, or to participate in research.